STAYING
ON TRACK

Lessons from a Customer-Focused
Travel Disruptor

FRANK MARINI

STAYING ON TRACK
Lessons from a Customer-Focused Travel Disruptor

© Frank Marini / railbookersgroup.com
Editor: Brett Peruzzi / PeruzziCommunications.com
Book Design/Art Direction: Levine Design / levinedesign.net
Cover photo: © World Travel & Tourism Council 2024

Library of Congress Control Number: 2024923156
ISBN: 9781941573754

Published by Damianos Publishing
2 Central Street, Studio #152
Framingham, MA 01701 USA
DamianosPublishing.com

Produced through Silver Street Media by Bridgeport National Bindery, Agawam, MA USA

Second Printing 2025

This book was printed on paper from sources committed to rigorous forest management standards, developing, and promoting sources of renewable energy, using recycled fiber and materials, and promoting forest certification in the U.S. and around the world. SFI (Sustainable Forestry Initiative), and FSC (Forest Stewardship Council).

(FSC Certification ensures that products come from responsibly managed forests that provide environmental, social and economic benefits to those forestry areas. The FSC Recycled label indicates that the product was made from 100% recycled materials.)

To my greatest fan, my mother, Beryl Marini.

Thank you for instilling in me the belief that anything is possible. Your unwavering support and love have been my guiding light. This book is a testament to your encouragement and the dreams you helped me chase. I am forever grateful and will always strive to make you proud.

"Frank and I are in the same business. Sure, my product is art and his is travel, but when you look closely, we are both providing 'customer-focused experiences.' Frank's book Staying on Track shows the importance of knowing who your customers are, and then customizing offerings based on what they 'actually' want, not what you think they want. Business owners often miss this point. Sometimes my art collectors say, 'Just paint whatever you think.' I can promise you the wild stuff that comes out of an artist's brain is not always what people want on their walls. We all need to learn to put the customer first."

Joe Everson, World's First Singing Painter

CONTENTS

ABOUT RAILBOOKERS GROUP

AS PRESIDENT AND CEO OF RAILBOOKERS GROUP, I like to say we take the complexity out of rail travel. It's something we've been doing for more than fifty-two years, and we continue to grow and innovate every day.

But what does that mean?

Let's say you've been dreaming of exploring Europe for a special anniversary with your loved one. Maybe you've got ancestral roots in Italy, while your spouse has always dreamed of seeing the Swiss Alps. And at the same time, you're seeing really good international flight deals to Charles de Gaulle Airport in Paris.

By the way, you don't speak a word of Italian, French or German, and you haven't ridden the trains in Europe since your twenties when you went backpacking with your college roommate.

Instead of the time, effort and frustration to piece it all together—one call to Railbookers connects the dots and takes care of it.

We specialize in independent rail-based vacations, which include train tickets, hotel accommodations, sightseeing activities, transfers, and much more. What we don't do is just as important—we won't just sell you a train ticket. Rather, we work with you via phone and e-mail to instantly create the perfect vacation.

And it doesn't just stop once we've taken payment from you. If you decide you want to splurge a little bit for a fancier hotel one night (we only book three-, four-, and five-star hotels) after thinking about it—we can do that. Want to surprise your spouse with an upgrade to first class? No problem. We work with our customers and travel agents every day to take care of their needs.

Best of all—we know things happen before and during travel, and that's why our 24/7 global support team is always available to deal with train delays and cancellations, rail strikes, weather emergencies ... really anything you can think of. You're jet lagged and you land in France to see a labor strike affecting some trains, but not all ... do you really want to spend hours on the phone to figure it out? Let us handle it instead.

Our Railbookers brand has thousands of itineraries across six continents, while we are also proud to be the official tour operator of Amtrak, Amtrak Vacations. There, we offer the same services and products using the United States' national rail operator—providing thousands of travelers each year the chance to ride the rails to America's national parks, biggest cities, and more.

In the coming pages, I'll give you a glimpse into a bit of the "secret sauce" that has made Railbookers Group grow wildly—before, during and after the global pandemic—and set us up for success into the future.

You'll see one common theme throughout—and that's an unending focus and obsession with the customer. After all, if we can't take care of them and provide world-class service, we won't be able to stay in business.

INTRODUCTION

IAM ORIGINALLY FROM RHODE ISLAND, and from an early age, I learned and understood hard work. I come from a very loving and hard-working family. My mother was a stay-at-home mom and my dad is an immigrant from Italy. He's a bricklayer, and neither of my parents attended college; my dad didn't even finish high school. But my parents were very much in favor of me and my brother getting an education and doing well. In high school, I ended up getting a job at a company called Collette Vacations, working in the mail room. In college, I became the marketing intern at Collette, and afterwards, I got into law school.

But I was still working for Collette, now in the marketing department. I had the chance to go on a familiarization trip to Kentucky (Tennessee and Branson), and that experience gave me all kinds of ideas. When I got back, I wrote a feedback memo to my manager, offering her ways in which I thought they should change the trip, and how that might make it better. That memo reached the CEO and, far from being offended, he liked what I wrote! He agreed with what I said, since my suggestions weren't based on what I liked, but on what I observed on the coach tour about what the customers thought, liked, said, and felt.

So, this put me on a path to a very different direction. I decided not to go to law school, but instead go into the travel business full-time. From that early stage, I was viewing everything from the point of view of the customer, and seeing things through their eyes. Those initial experiences were the basis of our data-driven business model today. Our work is a continuation of the work done by that kid who discovered that he had a knack for understanding customers' needs, wants, and continuous lessons; and if you pay attention to them, you know exactly what to do. It's still who I am today.

And I'm still learning. In 2016-17, I read *The Amazon Way* by John Rossman. I thought it was so good that I sent an email to the publisher, asking them to pass on my compliments to the author, and to let him know that it was one of the three best business books I had ever read. A week later, he emailed me and told me that he looked me up and discovered that we live near each other. He asked me if I wanted to grab a coffee! That was the start of a great friendship and relationship, where we got to know each other, and eventually I asked him to be the keynote speaker at one of our Railbookers Group Global Summits.

The questions he had for me about our company were really interesting. He didn't know anything about travel, but from a business perspective, he would ask me if I had thought about a given subject from this or that angle. He talked about when he worked at Amazon. At every meeting, Jeff Bezos had an empty chair, and he always said that the chair represented the customer. So, no matter what, customers were represented and had a voice in the meeting.

Ultimately, the customer's voice is always with us and around us.

That idea stuck with me, and now, it is a main focus of our company. How does this or that approach affect the customer? We listen closely to make sure that they have a voice in everything that we do. Our business is built around this practice, not just in our products and marketing, but the whole company.

〉〉 *How is your company, department, or role built around this idea?*

PUTTING THE CUSTOMER FIRST

❝ **RULE #1** - Customer Service is Not a Department
...Customer service is far more than a department name or a desk that shoppers or clients go to with problems and complaints. It's not a website, or a phone number, or an option on a prerecorded phone menu. Nor is it a task or a chore. It's a personal responsibility."

Lee Cockerell, *The Customer Rules: The 39 Essential Rules for Delivering Sensational Service*"

Fifty percent of the travel experience happens before you travel, which means you always have to ask a number of important questions:

- Who is your customer?

- Are you paying attention and interacting with them on a regular basis?

- Are you asking them key questions at every customer touchpoint in their journey?

This book will go into detail about what we do at Railbookers Group, what we've learned in our many years in the industry, and how our practices have benefited us and can benefit your business, to have a truly one hundred percent customer-led business model. I will pose questions to ask yourself for your business or department about how to truly be a customer-centric business.

Our business model is absolutely customer-led, and we believe there isn't anyone else like us who operates with this model. For us, *our customer creates the product*. When we first developed this business model, we were getting calls from potential customers, because we operated Amtrak Vacations™, and people wanted to customize their trips.

A lot of times people (even our travel advisors who purchase our products) will say something like, "We don't really have a lot of people asking for rail trips," and we always answer with the same response: "Neither do we. Our people are looking to travel. They aren't necessarily looking for rail trips." But they'll see the option and say, "Oh, I can do that by train! That's a lot easier!"

They might say, for example, "I'd like to go from Chicago to Glacier National Park, to Seattle, can you do that by train? How much does that cost, and how long does it take? Also, I want to do this with sightseeing, and stay at these hotels."

As we were creating customized itineraries for them on the fly, we began to observe the patterns, to see if people were asking for the same things. We could see a huge opportunity to attract new customers by studying what current customers were asking, saying, and quoting. What if we could create new customer packages based on what existing customers were customizing and then re-market those trips with a new name, images, maps, itinerary, and market on our website, in our emails, etc.?

We've obviously expanded our operations since then, but that model is still at the core of our work today. All of the products we have on any of our websites started from what we had already customized, created, and booked from our current customers. For example, we might see that, say, 726 people chose a particular products and services combination. This means that in a very real sense, we don't create our own product. The customer creates and drives the product development, and then we amplify and market it.

We bring that same philosophy into our marketing. We need to listen to our customers, not just market to them. It's amazing to me how many businesses today want to grow their business, get more customers, and expand to new segments, yet they don't really know, or actively listen to, or even speak to their current customers, the people who are paying their salaries.

For example, we've been doing webinars for ten years for potential customers. When people sign up for one of our webinars, we ask a series of questions about their potential vacation, and we're usually looking for answers in threes:

- What are the three things you're most interested in?

- What are the three things you're most excited about?

- What are the three most important things for you on this trip?

- What three things do you hope to gain from your vacation?

- What are the three places you'd most like to see?

- What are your three biggest concerns?

- What are your top three questions overall?

To be honest, these questions can challenge them a little, as they might not have thought about their vacation in these ways. A question about concerns or deal-breakers could even give them pause, as they might not have concerned themselves with any potential negatives up until now. However, these are the questions that need to be asked, since there are always negatives to any trip. For example, a customer might say, "I want to be in a hotel in the city center, and I want it to be walkable to everything." Okay, great! We can arrange that and they might have a big worry alleviated simply by us doing so.

If we ask them, "What are you nervous about?" they might answer, "I'm nervous about changing trains. I'm concerned about it in this station." No problem, we'll address that. They might ask us, "How is it to take my luggage on the train? How does that work?" We will show them exactly what to do.

The more they get into it, the more additional questions will come up, and we make the commitment to be with them, every step of the way. This structure also gives us great subjects for future webinars, blogs, and more. In one sense, our customers are also our marketing team. We try to understand what their excitement is, as well as their apprehension. These thoughts can be anything, and will differ from customer to customer. This way, we understand where a customer is coming from and what their hopes and concerns are, so we can highlight those and make sure to deliver on what's important to them.

But it doesn't end there. Our analysts then crunch that data and that information goes back to marketing to create content in the form of videos, blogs, downloads, guides, and new email subject lines. From this information, we also create new webinars based on what customers are asking for. So, everything in our product and marketing is customer-led, which is how we are able to truly grow, because we're aggregating these questions.

We need to be careful, though. People are consuming vast amounts of information these days, not just for their work, but in their daily lives. They scroll their phones constantly and so quickly that a lot of "big" information goes right by them. Being conscious of this, we tend to "drip" little bits of information to customers and potential customers, just enough to whet their appetites. You can't overwhelm people, so we use images and only a small amount of text to catch people's attention, enough to get them excited and wanting to know more.

Our work doesn't stop with those initial inquiries. We also continue to ask questions throughout the planning and booking process, as well as the customer's journey. And just as importantly, the company needs to keep questioning itself. Here are some important questions for any business to keep in mind:

- How often and in what ways are you asking your customers relevant questions?

- What methods are you using to reach out to them? Are you using a survey, or a phone call? Online chat? Another way?

- Are you doing this through the complete customer journey vs. just a post-purchasing survey?

- How are you tracking and measuring all the raw data answers to your questions throughout this journey to be able to analyze it or spot a trend?

More importantly, are you asking your customers questions about their experiences on regular basis:

- Before they become your customer?
- After they pay their deposit?
- Before their journey begins?
- During their journey?
- After their journey?

Our team has something called "Questions for Success," for when they're on the phone. They're asking key questions to gauge a customer's knowledge of rail, but also what's important to them, so we can make sure in their suggestions that we're recommending the right product or service.

I always give the analogy that we should think of ourselves like we're doctors. Imagine I went to see a doctor and when I walk in, he's not going to say to me, "Drop your drawers, I'll give you a shot, this will take one second."

No, he'll ask what's wrong, and maybe I'll tell him my stomach's been hurting for, say, three days. He'll ask me what I did then, and he'll try to come up with a diagnosis. In the same way, we're like "rail doctors." We ask the right questions, and then we're going to give suggestions, or maybe a choice of the three best packages and see what the customer wants, based on what they've told us is important to them. Honestly, a lot of companies just seem to offer one solution for all problems, but that can't really be the best way to operate.

I know I am speaking about a customer's travel journey, but this can be applied to any business on a customer's path to purchase. The reason we do this is because we'll get different answers to different questions along the way, and this will help us know how to improve our products and services, and also our booking and marketing messages. Sometimes we can answer their questions and offer our help and advice before they even ask. And that's taking service to another level! This process is constant, never-ending, and always changing. It can never end if we want to continue to improve and provide the best for our customers. We're constantly learning. Ultimately, some of the biggest questions any business needs to ask are:

- What do the customers want?
- What is the unmet need?
- What problem are they trying to solve?
- What information are they looking for?
- What information do they need that they don't even know to ask for?

It's rather surprising that these simple questions are often overlooked, leading to errors, mistakes, and individuals slipping through the cracks. We are committed to keeping that from happening. Ask yourselves, how do you do these things in your own business? The answers are always in the questions you ask.

Not long ago, I was in Nashville at a conference, which included one of our travel partners, with some of our wonderful travel advisors. Taking the time to meet with them, ask questions, and stay in the loop was of great help. As travel has opened up, it's important for us to keep up with the constant flow of information from customers, resellers, and potential customers, because they will tell us what's important to them and their customers at what time, and what products they need or are considering.

The reason we focus on this approach is that most people don't know a lot about train travel, even a good number of those working in the industry. Many see train trips as an old-fashioned way of traveling, especially across the United States, but there is tremendous potential there, even more so in Europe, Asia, and beyond.

One of the approaches that makes us unique is that we tend to target customers who are age fifty and over. Often people will ask us why we don't tend to market to Gen Z or to

Millennials. The simple answer is that they aren't buying our products. It's the fifty-plus customers that have the interest, the time, and the money. It's not that we don't want to serve these younger customers, we do and would love to do more! But at the end of the day, it goes back to the point: just pay attention to your customer. Who's buying it now? That's the gist. Too often, I see companies that want to grow their customer base, but they don't actually know who their best customers are, or why they buy. This is low-hanging fruit!

Our business model and approach might appear revolutionary these days. It seems like so many businesses are constantly telling customers what they "should" want, whether it's on streaming services, from book publishers, in entertainment, or travel: "Here is what you want to read, here's what we're putting on the radio for you to listen to, here's the show we're going to air," and so on. They do this instead of actually listening to what people want. It's astonishing how often this happens. In some ways, our philosophy is almost absurdly simple. A lot of companies seem to think that they know better than the people who are buying their product. We prefer to trust our customers, as it has served us well and continues to do so; we learn more every day.

Typically, if a company is investing so much in pre-production, or they worry if they get more margin on this or that product, they're going to push where they need help. With our model, we're really an aggregator of thousands of services, so at the end of the day, we don't need to emphasize a particular product that isn't working. There's no benefit to pushing one package over another, or trying to sell something that a customer doesn't want. We're not like a cruise line that has any number of dates that never sell, and says, "Let's push those so we don't take a loss." We simply don't have that issue, so it's a pure customer-driven focus.

What we find is that for any company, if you free your mind of those rigid ideas and you really focus on your customers' needs, they will actually tell you exactly what to do and what's important to them. Remember, you need to stay with them because their plans will change from time to time. Maybe they want to add a new destination, or it could be for any other reason, and you need to be there for them.

They might have seen an advertisement on television or read an article online, or watched a video or a TV show that has given them a new idea about what they want from their trip. It's true that all too often, customers easily get distracted, because they go for what they like, or they have a cost center they want to stay with, but being able to go along with those changes is how we built our business. And it works.

Put simply, you start with identifying who your customer is, and what they want and need, which seems simple enough.

But are you really paying attention to that?

Focus on where the customer can take you if you stay "on track." This is good advice for any business, of course, and it's worked for us.

You also need to remember that there are the realities in any travel excursion; not everything always goes right. A potential customer might wonder what happens if they miss a train connection. This is a legitimate concern. If someone is seventy years old, and something like this happens, that can be a serious problem. They don't necessarily know what to do. While there are no guarantees, our service tries to prevent these mishaps from happening to begin with. By planning out everything in advance, we can reduce some of the risk. Plus, we hedge for this by picking the best train times, having an emergency line, and monitoring all train delays.

It can be very difficult for someone to attempt to do all of this on their own. It can be quite a challenge if you're trying to figure out the complexities of travel, especially if you're going country to country and things don't always match up: different rail services, different currencies, different languages, and so on. On a country-to-country journey, which so many of our travelers like to take, they might have to deal with different train tickets. One ticket is in German, but the next is in Italian or French, and the station has different signs. How do they get to where they're going?

And yet, for our customers, they don't necessarily want to go on a structured, escorted coach tour with a large group. They want the freedom and flexibility to travel on their own, to choose their individual experiences; however, they might not have done this before. They don't want to have to, for example, drive in Rome; who does? They can choose the train, which goes right to city center, but then they might have apprehension about taking their luggage on the train or how early they need to get to the train station to check in.

So, when we ask our questions, it's with an understanding that there's always an interest in details and that our questions help them to navigate to the right product, the right service, the right everything. We're aware of trying to meet customer needs, precisely because we know that we might be just a part of someone's overall vacation experience. As an example, someone could be traveling to Europe and they'll want to take a river cruise. We don't focus on river cruising, but our customer might plan a river cruise that ends in, for example, Basel, Switzerland. Then, they'll book with us to go from Basel, down to St. Moritz for a few days, and then maybe to Lake Como and Venice. They don't want to rent a car, or find a bus service, but the train is a great option for them. For that portion of their journey, we strive to make everything go perfectly and take away any stress or concerns.

We want to get an understanding of what else they're doing on the whole trip so that we get a 360-degree view of the entire travel experience. Unfortunately, many times, a different vendor will only measure the portion of the trip they manage or fulfill, and they don't ask about or measure the customer's complete journey. They might not consider a particular hotel, what else the customer might be doing, how long they are traveling, and many other aspects of the overall vacation. Now, a travel advisor will know. And our resellers know that because they may be booking all those other aspects of the customer journey. We ask so that we understand their complete travel journey, even the parts they don't purchase from us. This helps us in identifying other products or services we could or should be offering, and it gives us a better understanding of what is important in our customer's overall trip.

❯❯ *How often in your business do you ask about the whole picture or journey?*

Our approach gets right back to the point I made earlier, in that we try to get the full view of what the customer is doing on their travel, which goes to the product standpoint. We use that travel information to help develop new products.

Here is one example: a number of years ago, my wife and kids and I were on one of our popular Amtrak Vacations™ trips and went from Chicago, via the Empire Builder overnight train to Glacier National Park, Montana, spending a few nights at the Glacier Park Lodge, and then back on the Empire Builder through the Cascade Mountains to Seattle, where we spent a few more nights sightseeing. It was a great trip! But along the way, I was in the dining car talking to some customers, and learned that they were not only doing that trip, but then they were going on an Alaska cruise afterward.

I asked, "When did you book the Alaska cruise?" (at the time we didn't offer our current Rail and Sail products to Alaska).

They said, "Oh, we booked the cruise first, but then we looked and decided that we'd always wanted to see Montana, we'd always wanted to go to Glacier National Park, so why don't we do a trip before our trip, instead of flying to Seattle or Vancouver? Let's fly to Chicago, take the train, and spend a few nights in Montana, in Glacier Park. We'll see the beautiful sights and then go to Seattle. So, it's a trip before the trip."

Continuing to learn from our customers, our product development team created Rail and Sail because of that experience. This whole part of our business came about simply by understanding these customers and why they did what they did. By asking a lot of questions, we really get to know our customers, and gain a larger view of what they're doing.

Our services are not limited only to the United States and Europe. We cover rail journeys in Australia, New Zealand, Asia, India, and Africa. Each of these nations and regions has its own unique rail system. There are the national rail systems, Amtrak, VIA Rail, Eurostar, SNCF, Trenitalia, etc., but then there are also specialty rail services, which are almost luxury lines. There is the Venice Simplon-Orient-Express, Rocky Mountaineer, Rovos Rail, and many more that we offer. Understanding different customers' needs, expectations, and why they are taking the trip is key.

We have customers that want to try out various aspects and pieces of a total trip. For example, we'll have customers that will fly to Europe and they'll go from Paris to Venice on the Venice Simplon-Orient-Express, but then they'll go to Venice, Florence, and Rome, on the Trenitalia rail system and visit these cities along the way. Our goal is to show potential customers another kind of freedom in travel, one that allows them to just sit back and enjoy the trip without the hassles of air travel or being responsible for getting yourself to your destination.

A lot of travel advisors have customers that want to travel, for example, around Europe. If they're not familiar with Railbookers, these customers have to go online themselves and book their rail tickets. In many cases, customers cannot book tickets until ninety, sixty, or even thirty days before the actual trip, even if they have contacted their agent a year in advance to book their vacation. They can book pretty much everything, except for rail tickets. So, that's where we found a huge opportunity in the market, not only with travel advisors, but also with their clients. With us, they can book up to two years in advance, and see the pricing and scheduling.

While rail travel is at the heart of what we do, it's really only a portion of what we do. We can book hotels of any kinds, sightseeing tours, meals, activities, transfers, and even ferries. Pretty much the only thing we don't book are flights, so as long as the travel advisor can book flights, we can take care of everything else, and really be the one-stop shop for the travel advisor and their customer.

OUR STORY

HOW DID WE GET TO WHERE WE ARE NOW? I'd like to talk just briefly about our history.

Our company started in 1972 and we have gone through many variations of corporate names, products, and the services we provide. If I fast forward to 2012, we had one office, one location in Beverly, Massachusetts, and eighteen employees. We focused on domestic rail travel, as the official tour operator for Amtrak, operating Amtrak Vacations™. It was in 2012 that we changed the train travel/Amtrak Vacations™ business model to allow our customers to be a product development team.

We took off with customers from the US and then internationally. One of those customers was Railbookers in the UK, who sold our Amtrak Vacations™ products. In 2016, we acquired Railbookers, and that's when we really started to go worldwide and offer rail vacations all over the world, including Europe.

OUR MODEL: REMOTE WORK AS THE STANDARD

WE MOVED FULLY TO REMOTE WORK in March 2020, and by the fall, we'd decided to make it permanent. I said to myself: "This is more efficient. We're going to get rid of our offices."

Previously, we had offices in London, UK, Beverly, Massachusetts, Laguna Hills, California and Sydney, Australia and our geographical locations tended to dictate our talent pool; who could we find in those areas? But now, we don't need to be concerned about that nearly as much. By going remote, we quickly recognized that there is a lot of great talent out there that we would never have had access to before. People might live in one place and not be willing to move to work in one of our offices, for example, but they would be perfect for one of our teams. Before they would have had to relocate, but now, they can stay where they are.

There were some wonderful people in our industry who lost their jobs, and I recognized that I could hire them because of the different destinations that were covered by my offices. So once again, we recreated ourselves and today, we have staff in six countries, thirty-four states, and all over the world. Honestly, we're much more efficient and effective with this new setup.

It might seem weird, but I would say that I was never really worried, because I could see us still trading, and I was always paying attention to our customer. I knew who they were, I knew where they were going, where they weren't going, and where they wanted to go. It was easier to recreate the company, because I was already ahead of where I could see it going. That was because I was having an ongoing dialogue with our customers, unlike those people that are so removed from their customers that they don't know what to do.

The remote advantage can't be overlooked as a major transformative step for the company. Our skeptics were quickly sold on the value of remote work when we realized that we could bring on amazing talent anywhere in the world that we couldn't have previously acquired. It's changed things in a lot of positive ways, including having access to more talent and a bigger hiring pool. Plus, our collaboration got sharper, as people from literally around the world could toss ideas back and forth. Though we've lost the "osmosis" of learning that comes from groups being together in a single place, our training team has done an amazing job in taking on that responsibility to be sure that our employees get the training they need, and that the ideas can still flow.

We're always looking at what works well in this new environment and we're excited for what comes next!

We also went from our local offices servicing the markets they are in to being a truly global company. Now, where you live has nothing to do with the work that you're doing for the customers we are serving. Now when we hire for a department or role, our first question is where on Earth should that role be based to ensure continuous movement and production. Say that a specific department works forty hours per week, five days a week, and was once all based in the East Coast of the US. Today, that same number of staff can be spread across six countries around the world.

People can call us from anywhere in the world, 24/7. We're responsive at all hours. Being a fully remote company and deciding to hire from wherever we needed resources, our responses are not just from an emergency or call center environment, but for every department. We might decide today that we need an accountant, or a software engineer. We decide where they should be to keep the machine going, which also provides extra customer service. So, when a customer calls about an issue, there's always someone to pick up and there's always a team that's available to answer whatever questions anyone might have.

Thus, everything can be taken care of and rebooked at that time. That's been a real benefit and made it very easy to scale. We are able to meet demand in real time with labor and support teams regardless of where the customer is or for what reason they are contacting or engaging us. We would have never been able to scale to the size we are today if not for being remote. We also can facilitate taking customers, not only customers who have a disruption, but also customers that want to book later in the day. We have people that maybe live on the West Coast, but they're night owls, and they want to call in at ten o'clock at night. They might get our Australian team in their morning time zone, and they can book with them. With our system, you can always get someone, whether it's on a query, after-you-book questions, or when you're on the trip.

And that just rolls across the Earth. Previously, we had offices across different regions, but we didn't have that service; everything was by market. So, for example, Australians called Australia. Different departments worked together, but not as one global company. But now, a team's location has nothing to do with the customers they're dealing with, and that's great! You don't want to have to staff a help line at two o'clock in the morning in San Diego, for example, just in case someone, somewhere needs to phone then. Literally anybody anywhere in the world can take a call if they need to and you've got people, all around the world at all times. Now if you are reading this and thinking, "Why don't they have an online booking engine vs. having to call or email Railbookers Group, it's because there is no online booking engine on Earth (or as I like to say, on the blue thing going around the yellow thing) that integrates all different rail systems, hotels, sightseeing activities, etc. But stay tuned for later chapters on what we are doing and what is to come.

We don't have to keep people literally employed twenty-four hours a day. They can work normal business hours, and just be in different places in the world. We find that being fully remote now and being strategic on where we're hiring means that the level of commitment, support, and positivity from our staff is amazing, because they appreciate the balance in their lives, and they can work from home and live wherever they want to live.

Employees are very supportive of our company's success and their own roles, and the opportunities they have, more so than I've ever seen before, simply because of what it provides them with personally. That makes me very happy. People are happier to stay in the long term if they have something that fits in with what they need in their personal lives, wherever they might be in the world.

We have employees who might say, "I'm in the US, but I've always wanted to go to southern Italy and spend a month there, so I'm going to do that. I'm going to work "x" amount of days, and I'll just work a later shift those days, then take a few days off. But now I can rent a home and take my family with me."

We've got people all over the world who take advantage of this benefit. It's no problem for us, just let us know. People can pick up and move anywhere in the world and still work for us, because they've just relocated to a new place. It doesn't really matter. And having that commitment so they can do that and have that lifestyle is really supportive of the company.

We'll say, "This task has to get done because we have a customer that needs it. But if you can do it in such-and-such a way, does that work for you?" And they'll say, "Great." They just appreciate having the conversation, so it's a win-win for everyone. They're glad if we can meet them halfway.

Working in a fully remote environment has been a new experience for us, and it continues to be, because we went from one to the other pretty quickly. As a result, we're always working on new ways to collaborate remotely.

Another creative way to thrive in a remote environment while ensuring productivity and holding onto our culture is that we have regular virtual coffee chats with cross-departmental staff to get to know each other. Many of our managers have weekly working sessions where the whole department is on video just working for two hours, but can see each other, ask questions, etc., to replicate being in the office.

We also have regional get-togethers which are working sessions, as well as our annual Railbookers Group Global Summit, where we bring in about one-third of our staff for meetings, trainings, and a "Fishbowl Session," where everyone is put next to each other in the conference room (arranged by department, more on this later) and works together for the day. Lastly, all staff submit to their managers, no matter what level, a "Mic" report, which is short for microphone. They fill in answers to three simple questions:

1. What observations, accomplishments, or learnings did you have this week?

2. What suggestions do you have for improvement on anything?

3. What is your goal to work on, learn, or accomplish next week?

It's a pretty simple process, but it's amazingly effective in a remote environment. For myself, I get mic emails from a wide selection of staff in each department at all different levels; it helps me get a picture of exactly what is going on in the company no matter where I am.

OUR TEAM

LET ME SAY SOMETHING ABOUT OUR TEAM. We've talked a lot about customers, but since we're such an employee-driven company, I want talk about those who work for us. Who are they? How do we hire them? What is their experience? What brings them to us? Who wants to work for us?

Honestly, we get more resumes than I can ever believe, partly because people are looking for something different; they don't want that traditional office experience. They want the flexibility of moving to wherever suits them. They actually want a fun job for a change.

They come from all different industries. Normally, we do get a lot of people from the hospitality and service industries, but we're also getting many more from other industries thinking, "You know what? I want to do something fun and something that's positive, and that allows me to work remote and have amazing travel benefits."

We get resumes from every background imaginable, and we hire from every background. As for our hiring process, it depends on the role. Obviously, we have some very technical positions, like software engineers, and these departments have to have certain criteria on, say, the financial side or the IT side. But in general, depending on the other roles, it's more broad-based in terms of someone's background and experience.

The person applying could be a travel agent, a teacher, a chef, or a fork lift operator. It doesn't matter. They're someone who's looking, who is interested and interesting, good with people, and loves the concept of travel. Really, they come from all over.

Our selection process is basically by position. We have assessments that they have to take: personality, to see who they are; basic technical knowledge, and so on. Then, we assess by the particular role, and this will include specific testing.

Once they've had their individual assessments, they'll go through interviews, usually a couple of rounds of interviews with the individual, the manager, or perhaps a couple of managers. Assuming that the aptitude is there, they're really looking for the right attitude. We are a very collaborative group of people. We're positive and we provide great customer service. We've turned away very bright, very talented people that we can see are not good at collaborating at all, which doesn't work in our environment.

No one person in the company, including myself, is that important. We need everybody. Where someone is not as collaborative, that doesn't mean outgoing versus more of an introvert. It's more if someone really doesn't want to collaborate, then we are not the right fit for them, because there isn't a department that isn't engaged with other departments. Is someone curious, or just an expert in an area? Because sometimes if someone is an expert in an area, they know what they know, but not what they need to know. We've turned down people because they just couldn't get along well with everyone. We might be a remote company, with all staff being remote, but that doesn't mean you work alone on an island. Quite the opposite.

We get people who are jumping from another industry, and really want to work in something that, frankly, is just more enjoyable. We have people from the financial industry, software and tech, even people who are business owners themselves.

These latter ones might want to try something new without all the stress that owning a business can bring. We also get a lot of referrals from staff; if someone likes working for us, there's a good chance they're going to recommend it to their friends.

Recently I was meeting with our recruiting team, asking about how it was going, what are they hearing from candidates, etc. They told me about how people had read about us, seen our videos, and so on, and said to them, "That's the kind of company I want to work for. I see all the diversity you have, all the different ages, ethnicities, and everyone having fun and hugging each other. Like, you guys get along and like each other, and have fun while working. This is where I want to work and be engaged."

And that's who we are. You must be like that or honestly, you can't work in travel; it just doesn't make sense. It's a hospitality thing, and the whole point is customer service; great customer service starts internally. Now, that doesn't mean we don't have "robust" dialogue and debates about things, but ultimately, it's all about how we give better service to each other.

We offer a fun environment. It's not like we're talking about widgets all day long. We're talking about something you get to see and taste and touch, and everyone says, "Ooh, when do we go there?"

Another quality we look for is that we absolutely make sure that someone loves change. We change so fast because we follow the customer, as you've seen. That's how we develop product and how we market. Some people don't like change, so they struggle in that environment. People that tend to fall in love with their own ideas and can't let them go can really struggle in this environment. But as always, it's not about them, it's about the customers.

That being said, the team that we do have very much em-braces change and new ways of doing things. They'll find the nuggets and the new ideas, and they realize that they can take one, put it in here, put that messaging out there, and see if that works. It's very fulfilling to them that they paid at-tention, took something, amplified it, and then they see the result.

The people that appreciate this approach—being all about change—also really thrive with us, as opposed to those that say, "No, just tell me what to do, and I will do that single func-tion all day long."

But we don't create static products. Our products change based on what the customer wants them to be, and if you get into that, it's very interesting. So, our employees get engaged with it. That adaptability is so important, but I think so many businesses fall down with that part of the work. They do get in that rut of, "This is the way we've always done it, and it works, so let's not rock the boat."

But embracing the fact that the company, even the indus-try, is going to be different in a year, or even in a few months, is a huge thing. You not only have to embrace it but come to love it.

I think that's why a lot of businesses fail, because they don't embrace changes (big or small). They get stuck, and when something gets too rigid, it breaks or they just fall in love with their own idea and push to make it work. But if you can bend and be flexible with the proverbial wind, then you're going to be around longer; we appreciate that idea. We are thankful that we re-engineered our business model around our customer and what the product can be. We embraced the customization and flexibility while ensuring they are scalable.

PRODUCT DEVELOPMENT

FOR PRODUCT DEVELOPMENT, we take a similar approach. We need to know what products our customers are looking for and why. We study the patterns that we see and then work to customize a travel package for them, but we are always looking at how we can enhance that. From the start, we want to know two things:

- **First, how did that customer get to that point?** In other words, why did they want that specific destination, hotel, sightseeing, attraction, or product? Is it a destination they've always wanted to visit? Is it something that they read about or saw on a TV show? Did they hear about it from a friend or a neighbor that went on a similar trip? Did they see it on social media? Is our trip an add-on to a longer trip? A post-cruise trip? And so on. Ultimately, what's the thing that is important to them about that product?

- **Second, what are the experiences that they want to have when they are there? What are the "must haves?"** Is it the customer that says, "Okay, we're going to Venice, I want to have a gondola ride"? Or maybe the customer says, "No, I want to visit some of the historical sites instead." It doesn't matter. Whatever the experience that they want, that is the one that's important to them *and* to us. How can we continue to enhance our products and services based on what that customer is looking for? And does that destination deliver on that promise?

On our side, knowing that there are more than 26,000 rail stations in Europe, the possibilities are as far and wide as the imagination can take the customer, because the infrastructure is already in place. Incredibly, in 2022 alone, over one billion people traveled on trains just in Europe!

Even in the United States, Amtrak goes to forty-six of the forty-eight contiguous states, so a customer can go to so many places—often wherever they'd like—and stop along the way. Is their destination the final stop, or is it a trip before a trip, like what we offer in Rail and Sail? Or maybe it's a place along their designated route. It can be anywhere the customer didn't know about previously (or maybe they did), and decides that they want to include it on their itinerary.

If the customer has something specific in mind, we can offer suggestions: "Since you're going that way anyway, here's something else you might like, because this dovetails with your interest in such and such. Maybe you'll want to stop off for a night in a little town in Italy that has a fantastic food festival. You could stay there for the night, and then head on to Florence the following day." We should always be looking for the extras and the bonuses that can turn a run-of-the-mill vacation into something truly special.

This is what we do from the product standpoint; for us, it's very exciting. The members of our product development team love their jobs, even though they don't necessarily create all the product designs themselves—again, the customer does—but they get to see these patterns all the time, learn why the customers want to go there, and how they can improve the product or service.

As we've mentioned, customers might have seen a destination, hotel, or train experience on a TV show or online, or they read about it in a magazine article. They might not even have known anything about that particular travel option before, but now, they want an add-on because of something in a given area. And we love that! It's always exciting to see a new place, a new destination, a new stopover that's coming from a customer that we may not even know about! What's up with that town? Oh, that's great, we'll add that to our future recommendations. So, our customers can help us, just as we help them.

And of course, the communication doesn't end with the customer booking the journey and going on their way. We always solicit their feedback during and after the trip. After a customer puts down their deposit, we send them another survey, with the same concept as the initial one, asking them again about the three things they are most looking forward to, the three things they are most concerned about, and so on. Then we survey them post-trip, when they come back. We'll ask them various questions, such as:

- What are the three things you were most surprised about?
- What were you most excited about?
- What exceeded your expectations?
- What things would you change?
- What didn't meet your expectations?
- What would get you to do it all again?

We do this to better fine-tune the product. In a very real sense, they have "created" the product themselves, but our job then is to make it better for both repeat customers and new customers.

These post-vacation surveys can be very revealing. If we start hearing the same things over and over again, that's very important, both for positive and negative responses. If we start hearing not-so-great things about one particular town or attraction, we can quietly drop that destination or experience off the recommendation list. Perhaps the hotels are noisy, or they all have poor service; if so, we won't recommend them in the future. We are always fine-tuning the experience to be better.

Nothing stays the same; it's the way of the world. Things change in destinations, or maybe we find out that a customer had a logistical problem. There might be construction, or going from point-to-point, they couldn't get where they needed to on time. Or perhaps some disruption prevented them from sightseeing. We want to stay ahead of these things to help us when making future recommendations.

We also want to make our business the best it can be, hence all these surveys and feedback.

- Is that decision good for the customer?
- Does that choice make sense?
- How do we make it better?
- How do we make it so it's easy (or easier)?

We constantly have to tweak our practices and make sure not to rest on our laurels in any way.

And from the marketing standpoint, our marketing is also built on this philosophy, which we'll get into in more detail later on. We have lots of customer data from our surveys and webinars, since we are a data-driven and data-forward customer-first company. All of this data provides us with different ways that we can measure those customers' voices and what they're thinking about. We need to be able to answer their questions so we can see the pattern of the questions, and then can create the content that answers them.

As an example: One of the biggest things we would see a while back was people asking what it's like to travel overnight by train. If they're traveling in the United States with Amtrak Vacations™, how would it work with luggage, sleeping, dining, the bathroom, and other facilities? In response, we created a series of "What's it like to overnight on a train?" webinars, as well as guides and videos for potential customers.

We explain to them that really, the train is their hotel, transportation, and restaurant all at the same time. But what is the beginning-to-end experience like? Do they have to get to the train station two hours early and go through security like an airport?

We've built that information in and we have downloadable guides. They can download the guide, and get the answers they need. What does overnight travel really look like? What will they see and experience? And in the surveys that we send to them after they come back, we'll put their answers into the marketing points: here's what our customers say they love about this trip or that destination, or why you simply must take the train if you're going to Switzerland. Why would you drive?

Indeed, in the Alpine regions of Europe, you'll see things that you couldn't possibly see by car; it's incredible to experience the train ride through there. Switzerland in June can be as amazing as Switzerland in January. One will give you the landscape covered in snow, the other covered in a carpet of green.

But we always need to be mindful of who's taking these trips. When a business is talking about potential customers, as we've noted, obviously the first question is: Who is our customer? It's important that we identify them. Who's most likely to want to take a train trip? And again, we've found that the majority of travelers who come to us are aged fifty and over.

But it's important to understand that these are not "senior citizens" in the way that people have traditionally thought of people in that age group. These are the Gen X and late Boomers who often consider themselves to be more worldly and knowledgeable. Many of them will come to us with a good sense already of what they want.

But they are very different from each other because it's still a lesser-known mode of transportation, so we see a wide variety within this group of travelers. We find in our key customer groups that they are traveling for different reasons. It's not the same from customer to customer.

Many people ask me, "Are your travelers train enthusiasts or train buffs?" I always answer, "Not at all. Think of it this way: are all the passengers on a given flight plane enthusiasts or airline buffs?" At the core, we are a mode of transportation that connects people and places. But of course, we are so much more, so the reasons our guests travel with us can be very different, even unique to each customer.

What we notice is that while many customers are over fifty, they don't consider themselves to be over fifty in the way that people might have twenty or thirty years ago. They are not from the World War II Generation; they were the "cool kids" from the 1970s and '80s. They will tell you that they still feel like they're in their thirties inside, despite what their outer selves might say! They listened to Led Zeppelin in the '70s, or Metallica in the '80s, or Nirvana in the '90s, and they've done things their parents might never have done; a lot of things! They don't really care what "the kids" are doing today with their own youth-focused travels; they want something different for themselves.

Many have been across the United States, or lived abroad; maybe they've studied at a foreign university for a year or more. A lot of them have already traveled much more, and seen different parts of the world. They are not a part of the so-called senior citizen crowd and don't see themselves that way.

This is the big difference between them and their parents or grandparents at their age, who probably didn't travel as much. Because of that, the idea of rail travel is more appealing to them; it might even be a novelty. They can have some apprehension or fear, but honestly, there isn't as much, certainly not like what their parents or grandparents would have had in their day. The idea of experiencing different languages and cultures, different countries and new people is already interesting to them. They're much more adventurous, which immediately lends itself to traveling by train for a vacation or an adventure. They don't want to be restricted to a set group or a set of rules, because they've already traveled. They have that excitement to try something new, so it's a different experience for us when we work with them. We don't have to "sell" the product quite as much if there isn't that apprehension; it kind of sells itself. We like to say with Railbookers Group and rail travel, your journey begins the second you step on board the train.

And to be honest, for our customers who are in their sixties and seventies, if we call them "seniors," they would respond, "We're not that old!"

It's all about perception, and even their perception of what a senior is can be very different from those of previous decades of travelers. They might object: "I'm not a senior, I was at Woodstock!" There is such a generational gap that came along in the 1960s with the way people perceive aging and where they are in their lives at a given time. Speaking as someone who is over fifty, who recently got my AARP card, and who loves heavy metal, I get where they're coming from!

It's an interesting phenomenon to observe. Everyone these days likes to think, "No, we're not old!"

This means we have to be mindful of this when putting together trips for them. Many people are much more willing to do adventurous things than the same age group might have done twenty years ago, when just sitting by a hotel pool might have been enough. Now, more people want to get out and really experience the place they're visiting, and we're only too happy to help them.

It's worth addressing that there's a different perception among these groups of what travel can be. For many of our parents or grandparents, travel was much more expensive, for example. If they were in the US, they went on road trips. The idea of going to Europe and railing in Europe wasn't what a lot of people did. People in the 1970s, the latter-day hippies, would find their own ways across Europe. Think of the hippie guy who just hitchhiked and took cheap rail across the continent. He's a little older than our main customer base, but already there was beginning to be a shift in perceptions about travel, which we're really seeing now.

For those who have experienced other cultures in their youth, they bring a different perspective to their travels now. They might have had an inside view of cultures in a way that people don't get if they're just visiting Paris and seeing the Eiffel Tower. A lot more people that are looking at these kinds of trips with us are going to be of that mentality. They've had special experiences. Maybe they lived in Tokyo for a year, or they stayed in Berlin for six months. There's a more worldly sense in these generations than might have been the case before.

Travel is the great equalizer for education, and for gaining new perspectives on different people and different cultures, as well as being willing to have more than just one viewpoint on things, and we definitely see that attitude with our customers. They love that, as all of us who travel do. We love the different experiences and meeting different people, and travel provides that.

There's more to it than just seeing the Eiffel Tower in Paris or Big Ben in London; it's a chance to get inside a culture, maybe learn a little of the language, eat the local foods, see how other people live. People can choose to spend the night in a place that's out of a main town, perhaps in a little villa or a small B&B; there are more of these opportunities than ever before. Some of people's most enjoyable travel experiences around Europe and the world are things like that, the little experiences away from the big tourist draws.

Someone can use our service to make a stop in the countryside that a bigger travel package might not include. It gives them a chance to wander about and even slow down the pace of their vacation; it is supposed to be a vacation, right? People can revel in wandering the twisty-windy streets of a medieval town in Italy or France, where there's nothing in particular to see, certainly not what a "typical" tourist might be interested in. But in doing so, they get a feel for a whole new world. They might be in a Tuscan hill town, just sitting outside a café and eating gelato. They might not understand a word of the language, but they're experiencing something new and amazing. The traveler sees that this is what the locals do: they gather in the town square at noon, they converse, they play chess, they talk about the state of the village or the region, all while letting the afternoon hours pass by in a leisurely way. People can see things that aren't in the guidebooks. For a day or two, they can step into another world, and it really does give a different perspective on things. We strongly encourage these kinds of extras and love building them into a trip from the beginning.

Some of our customers might already have done things like this, had these unique experiences, and they come looking for more. They want to journey beyond the big sites. They don't want Big Ben; they want a day or two on a sheep farm in the Cotswolds. They don't want the city center and the busyness of Paris; they want a fishing village on the coast of Brittany. They're a little more of what we might call the "next stage" of traveler. They're excited about the possibilities that rail travel opens up for them. They're a little different.

And of course, we also have the customer who is an American traveling just in the United States. Maybe they are just beginning their travel journey; it could be a shorter trip, or one combined with a flight or a cruise somewhere, but they're not as aware of just how much of America they can see and visit by train. If we have a customer from the UK or Australia visiting the US, we might find that they're looking for famous journeys, like taking Route 66.

So regardless of whether they are traveling in the United States or abroad, we may have a customer that, as mentioned, views the rail journey as just a "trip before the trip." We might have a customer that has the option to fly to get to a destination, but they don't want to fly and don't want to drive, so they'd rather take a train. We might have a customer for whom this is a bucket list experience; they want to try something different. They might be approaching train travel as if it's like a plane, where everyone on the plane is going to the same locations, but for different reasons. They bring that same concept to the train, but the one thing that's common among them is that they're actually looking forward to traveling by train!

The idea of a train journey often brings smiles to their faces, because it's different from a plane in several ways.

A customer might prefer the train to flying for any number of reasons. They might be afraid of flying, or maybe turbulence makes them freak out. Maybe they get air sick, maybe they hate the whole tedious process of navigating through an airport (who doesn't?), and with a train journey, they don't need to worry about any of that.

They also don't need to worry about driving in a location they don't know, and they don't have to think about being herded along in a large group on a tour bus. A bonus: they get to enjoy a meal, a drink, look out over amazing scenery, or even just read a book.

Best of all, often, they're going right into the city center. They're not flying into Charles de Gaulle Airport in France from Heathrow Airport in the UK. They can just travel from St. Pancras station in London to Gare du Nord in central Paris. They're in town, saving time and effort, so they can get on with what they want to do. And some European cities really do put you right in the middle. We're always reminded of Cologne in Germany, where you step off the train and the incredible Dom cathedral is right there, as you exit the station. It's fantastic!

These are some of the many reasons customers buy from us. However, there are also benefits we see on the post-trip, and many first-time customers become repeat customers.

So, when we consider our customers, we need to understand that they are quite varied and different. What we would say to any company, whoever your customers are: *Really get to know them, and what they're doing on this trip.*

Ask those questions and learn more. Each customer is so different from every other one. What are those differences? Why are they interested in that particular product? Learn about what makes them unique, but also look for any commonalities, between them, and you'll begin to notice patterns. Are they looking for something exciting, different, or fun? Or is their journey simply one from point A to point B?

The train trip can be an experience in and of itself, which is nice, since driving can feel like drudgery and flights can be tedious, especially if one is doing short flights within Europe. Often, it's such a hassle. A person needs to go to the airport and do the security check-in, the baggage check-in, and so on. Many of the local European carriers have severe restrictions on, for example, the amount of luggage one can bring (even with carry-ons), before they start charging for every little thing. It has been a source of irritation and annoyance for European travelers for many years. The airline might advertise a trip from Paris to Naples for only €20, but then the add-ons start—luggage, carry-ons, even food—and soon, your "bargain" ticket has ballooned up to €150 and you're feeling ripped off. It's supposed to be a pay-as-you-go option, but all too often, it just feels like a bait and switch, leaving one wondering if they should have considered a train trip instead.

Due to environmental concerns, France is trying out a new ban on some domestic flights to reduce emissions, meaning that more people will have to take trains. There won't be flights allowed under a certain distance, so that lends itself to train travel, which is the intention. Indeed, this new law will undoubtedly lead to an increase in the number of train departures available to meet the extra demand.

I recall how, back in 2019, I was in Berlin for a conference and the day I was scheduled to fly back to London, the airline went on strike! Undaunted, I just changed my plans and booked a train to go back to London instead. I took Deutsche Bahn from Berlin to Cologne, and then on to Brussels. From there, it was easy to change to the Eurostar back to London. In total, it took about eight hours, but I got so much work done, had a great meal, got to see beautiful sights along the way, and it was smooth and stress-free.

When one starts to add up the time allotted for flying—getting to the airport at least two hours ahead of time, checking luggage, the flight itself, landing, waiting at customs and immigration, retrieving luggage—it's honestly not much of a longer trip. The hassle is often considerably less, and the trip itself is often far more pleasurable. This kind of train journey can be a much more efficient use of one's time, even if it takes longer.

Whether your trip is for business or a vacation, the train offers numerous advantages. Of course, flying is the only option for distant locations, such as San Francisco to Sydney, or London to Hong Kong, but once you arrive, if there's a rail network at your disposal, the possibilities are almost limitless! And we always want our products to reflect that.

If you look at the way a lot of people develop product in the travel industry, it's very expertise or feel-driven, meaning someone might talk to the tourist board in a given destination and they'll hear that a certain product will be "hot" next year. Therefore, the company should think about promoting that product in anticipation. Sometimes, you can stumble onto a travel gem this way, but you're betting all your marbles on that, because you might be working on a package that's two years out from the current date. If you're wrong, you're gambling a lot and could lose, because you're not basing your product on what the customer wants, you're basing it on educated guesses, hunches, and hopes, or what another industry expert is telling you. You'd better hope you're right, or your guesswork might all be for nothing.

The reality is that every single week, our product development team is working with our analytics teams, crunching the numbers and dissecting every variation and modification to a product. It's all independent travel, which is great for us, since it means we can modify and customize anything. We can take that standard Rome-Venice-Florence trip and move things around, flip them, add extra nights, extra sightseeing excursions, add another city to the itinerary, etc.

We constantly analyze website hits, keywords, what agents have quoted, how they modified a package, and how frequently a given combination of travel options has occurred. It's an exercise in paying attention to customers' needs, as well as in pattern recognition. The customer is already going to tell you what's going to be "hot" next, because they are modifying it to their wishes in real time. We see those modifications and changes as opportunities to bundle up new packages, and we can get them marketed and out to potential other customers in twenty-four to forty-eight hours. Yes, that quickly.

During the worst days of COVID-19 (summer of 2020), when the world was effectively shut down, our product development team launched 171 new itineraries, pulling in a significant amount of money at a time when most agents were getting nothing. We were receiving daily bookings and launching new products almost constantly. We were able to find what was working at the time, and add incremental revenue just by listening to what customers were saying to us indirectly. We were able to keep feeding new products into the pipeline that kept on generating revenue at a time when it might have seemed impossible.

Nevertheless, what works in one year might not work in the next, and it will need to be modified or replaced altogether. Yet this isn't a hindrance; this policy is a never-ending source of inspiration and great ideas.

We like to say: *Great products are not invented, they're discovered.*

We don't actually come up with the ideas so much as we find them, and we know how to find them the right way. So, even during the 2020 shut downs, we knew that people were already excited about future travel, and we had that going for us. But surprisingly, we found that people were traveling every day, even then. Believe it or not, we took new bookings every single day throughout that year. Some were for 2021 or 2022, but many were also for 2020. We were more fortunate than many of our competitors, but it wasn't due to luck, it was due to our always paying attention.

We found that by focusing on what was important to customers, we were able to keep bookings coming in throughout the year. We know of tour operators who took in literally no money for 2020 and even for 2021. That's a pretty dire situation! By contrast, we were already on the upswing and into recovery by the fall of 2020, thanks to our approach. It was a testament to a good product and that we listened to what was resonating with our customers. It made a huge difference for us.

At a time when no one wanted to be stuffed on coaches with forty people, or on a cruise ship, or on an airplane (if you could even find a flight you could afford), trains—especially in North America and Europe—had another option: the private sleeper car. You could travel on board by yourself (or with your family, for example) and not have to come into contact with others. We recognized that we had an opportunity. A lot of people who were determined to travel saw that they had a way that they could do so and still feel safe.

During that time, people traveled locally, that is, in their home countries. Our American customers visited national parks and other local locations, as did those in Canada. Our UK customers were buying tons of trips to England and

Scotland. They were using the rail services to get to places in their own backyards. People realized that local destinations were great places to visit and that we had those packages already. So, for example, we asked ourselves, what would Scotland look like to someone living in England, versus someone going there from America? What did we need to modify? And we did need to make some adjustments, but the infrastructure was already there, as were those customers that wanted to take advantage of it. All of our markets across the world were still eager to travel, they just did so closer to home, so we pivoted to work with that.

This practice helped us from a credibility standpoint, as well. Some big companies and tourist boards were out there trying to reinvent themselves, to do anything they could to keep afloat when the hard times hit. It was quite a struggle and one could definitely feel for them. Since we already had everything in place—the partnerships, the rail lines, the hotels—we just redirected customers to different places for a period of time, or we sold more of what was already working, such as parks and such. The speed at which we were able to move and offer new packages also helped us tremendously.

Even now, people are still using our services for more local travel: Americans to national parks, the English to Scotland, and so on. But of course, things have shifted back to more "normal" as people now want to book more flights to destinations farther away. We then step in and accommodate their needs just as easily, as we've always done.

Now, people are ready to go out again and trying to find ways to get there! If anything, the travel numbers are up from pre-COVID-19 times. Italy was always busy, for example, but now it's really busy! The situation looks more like 2019, with some interesting variations for what people are now doing with their travel plans. The desire for travel will always remain.

PRODUCT STANDPOINT

FROM THE PRODUCT STANDPOINT, the product is as far and wide as we want to take it with all the large rail systems and networks. Every week, we look at how we're creating product, but we're also engaging ourselves on a regular basis to see what else is developing—the volume, what's interesting—in those destinations, in those areas. What are people going to?

One of the things that we'll do is have our product team be on the ground. They're traveling a lot and they're in those destinations, and they will be meeting with our vendors, the hotels, and the sightseeing attractions. But what they're also doing is talking to people in the lobby. They're talking to people at the piazza, they're sitting down and asking people where they're from. They're doing market research on their own while they're in the location: "I saw those people, they didn't travel with us, but this is why they travel, this is what they're looking for, this is what they were doing."

We're constantly investigating what else we can add to enhance our product, particularly if someone's going to this destination, they don't want to be on a bus tour, and they're traveling by rail. As mentioned, we do surveys on this situation and ask:

- What else are they doing in that destination on their own?
- What did they book or plan on their own?

We incorporate that information, ask those questions, and get that feedback from our product team. We're on the ground surveying and doing it.

And that's always fun from a product standpoint, just to see what we can put in, because that gives us a lot of marketing might. We could ask a customer if they know about a particular attraction, and we'll offer to include it. By doing this, we can evolve on a regular basis, we can see what's being customized, what's being booked often, what the patterns are, and then put all that out there for our customers. That's our product cycle.

Another thing about the product cycle, outside of what we do: We always study where there's new airlift going, because if there's an airlift going somewhere, typically passengers are following. Airlines will put flights on to a location if they see a pattern of travel, so we study that. We might see that, say, American Airlines has over a given week, 1,000 people that are going to this new destination all of a sudden. What do we have there? They are probably running air specialist deals, but what do we have there on the rail side? Is there a product that we can put out there? We might notice that there's a lot more lift coming into one destination versus not as much lift going somewhere else. Why? What changed? We've got a better shot of improving our own services if people are going there, anyway.

There has been a real shift post-COVID-19 as you can imagine, down and back up, but that was the pattern we followed before, and we're following it now, too, but it's still shifting as things open up. If one destination gets hotter over another, they'll open a secondary, which means we always have to keep an eye on that, too.

When we study where people are traveling, we see that the majority of the journeys are between Europe and North America; and our staff is spread out between both. But people are also going to Asia and Australia, of course. These locations are the primary ones.

We also find that some of our most popular destinations lend themselves to the train, because they're hard to get to by any other means. For example, whether it's Glacier National Park, or the Cinque Terre in Italy, there's no airport there and the bus isn't very good, either. This is where we come in and offer up alternatives, such as the option to stay right in one of the five villages in Cinque Terre, or the traveler can stay right at Glacier Park lodge, so here's the enhancement to the product, but all by train.

We have to be aware that on the product side, we can get lost in product because there's always a vendor, a tourism board, and so on, that will want us to work with them. But at the end of the day, we can't work with everyone. We have to make sure of what our customers are asking for, where they are going, where do we see people movement, etc.

Even here, we have to be selective about some things. It's not that we don't want to offer everything, but we have to be mindful of how much we want to market certain things, based on volume, ROI, and where there is already a trend. That one small area of that one location might want us to market their product, or list it, but honestly, nobody's asking for it and it's off the beaten path, or it's hard to get to. So, while we might have some people who will go there, it's a very small number. Maybe they read a great book from a writer years ago, who talks about their adventures in that town or region, but only a small amount of people who have read that book or want to go there; they're not the majority. As much as we'd like to include every destination and every option, we simply can't.

Still, there might be some options for including lesser-known, off-the-beaten-path locations. What we try to do is offer things up that are different. We might say to ourselves, "Hey that's a really cool town, but you know what? It won't market or sell on its own, so let's connect it to these other more appealing places, the ones that are more mass market, and advertise this place as just a stopover on the way."

We know people might come back and say, "That was amazing! We weren't expecting anything from that!" But to market it on its own sometimes doesn't have enough juice, because it doesn't have enough notoriety, or it's too difficult to get to. We always consider the balance between the heavily visited areas and the lesser-known destinations that might really be special if we can just find a way to get people there and back without any difficulties. We can put some locations in our offerings that are different. An example would be Cinque Terre in Italy, which is amazing but very few would go there only, versus visiting other amazing cities and towns in Italy, or places that we can't give full force of marketing to because they wouldn't stand on their own.

For those who are lucky enough to get to travel often, and have visited a variety of places around the world, they know differently. Whether for business or pleasure, people often find that we have more in common than we might think with those we meet. What's fascinating to me is that in every place that I've been to, I find most people are actually the same. Everywhere I go, they're kind, they're nice, they're all about family. They want their kids to do well, to be educated. I've been everywhere from Israel to Jordan to Egypt; I was in Riyadh in Saudi Arabia last year. I've also been all over Europe, and I just find that there are so many more commonalities between people than differences. It's very interesting.

I am lucky enough to be a member of the board of the World Travel & Tourism Council (WTTC). At one of our conferences, I was sitting at a table with a new group from all over the world. Next to me was a lady that runs a travel company; she's British, but lives in and runs her business out of Italy. Next to her was another lady who's originally from Mexico

City but lives and works in London. Two other women next to me were from Saudi Arabia and represent Saudi Arabian tourism. Next to her was another woman who was from the Philippines, but who now lives in Dubai. And then there was me, the only American in our immediate group.

We were having a quick conversation and so someone asked me, (which I thought was great): "As an American, do you drive a big truck and have guns?"

And I said, "No, why do you ask?" She replied, "We thought everyone in America did."

I asked her if she had been to the US to visit, to which she replied no, and I said, "You should visit, as we would welcome you there." But isn't that the stereotype of everywhere outside of the United States?

I then said to the Saudi women, "You can't drive, right?"

They laughed. "No, we can drive!"

And the lady from the Philippines who lives in Dubai said, "Everyone asks me if I can go to the beach and wear a bikini? Of course I can!"

They were all giving what they were getting from perceptions. It was a fascinating conversation for all of us.

It was a very interesting conversation about travel being the great educator and equalizer, and whatever someone had as a perception about other places. What we were all saying was, "Have you been there? Do you know anyone from there? Have you actually seen it? Where are you getting that information from? Is it through a lens?"

I'm not saying these preconceptions are all right or wrong, but when you get to meet people, they're interesting, regardless of where they're from.

Travel is an equalizer. It breaks down those barriers. The people coming to our service are going to be the kind of customers who already have that attitude and want to experience new things. They're adventurous. They'll want to take a side trek to a small town in India or go for a walk in the mountains, for example.

When we think of our customers, we tie it back to that sense of adventure. Sure, they will want some creature comforts, but at the end of the day, they're going to experience something different than they have at home; if not, they would just stay at home! Because if you're going to experience the exact same thing, why did you pay to go there?

This is not an issue we are overly concerned with, but we all know about how so many people used to book seven days at a hotel in Hawaii or Mexico, for example, and literally just stay at the hotel and the pool. Well, you could just go to a hotel in your hometown and sit by the pool. So why not get out and do something else, something different?

The attitude toward travel and vacations has changed a lot over the last say, twenty to thirty years. Sitting quietly used to be the thing people loved doing, but now so many people want more than that. Our customers are more adventurous. They want to see and do things. Our offerings give customers a journey in and of themselves, not just a destination. From a product standpoint, that's what we want to offer!

CONTACT STANDPOINT (DIALOGUE VS. MONOLOGUE)

WITH EVERY FUTURE GUEST, customer, or travel advisor, we need to know how much contact they want from us, in what way, and when. Some people have a lot more questions than others. Some people want to know what's coming up, how to better understand the documents they need, what things to look forward to, and so on. That may involve pre-buying versus post-buying, researching, downloading guides, finding out more, having videos sent out, and explaining things in detail, on-trip to post-trip.

As a result, we have to decide how often we need to reach out to our customers in a way that's right for them, in the way they want to be communicated with or updated, how often, and in what format. And we're always challenging ourselves in different formats.

As we grow and scale, we need to adapt to our customers' preferred means of communication. We want to communicate with them in any way that they want to communicate, not how we want to communicate. Sometimes they just want to keep things simple, which we can accommodate. The number of ways to communicate in today's world can be daunting: phone, email, video conference, social media, online chat, text, WhatsApp, etc.

Here are some of our main questions to whoever's reading, whether it be a travel agent, an advisor, or another business:

- Have you asked your customer how they want to communicate with you and in what ways? Give them more than just an opting out of an email option.

- Is there a better way that's scalable, but also profitable?

- And at the same time, can you provide world-class service, so someone feels right up to date?

- And what is that content and contact that you're providing? What's really helping them?

Here's another example of good communication: A couple of years ago, my brother and his family wanted to rent an RV, take the kids, and drive around the United States. They'd saved up for it. When he told me about it, I told him it was an awesome idea! But I then said to him, "Jim, you're not the best driver. You're going to rent an RV? You don't even know how that stuff works."

Hey, he's my younger brother so I can say that to him!

He said to me, "No! After I booked, they sent me information called 'first time campers.' It's a short directory, but it's got small clips of videos on how to hook up the electric, how to do all this other stuff, and they tell you exactly what to do. So by the time you're ready to go, you pick it up and they'll show you. It's not the first time you've looked at it."

And I'm thinking, that's genius!

That experience led to our discussion about this practice as a potential method of delivering information to our customers. What are the questions our customers ask? What are they apprehensive about? What could we put together after they book with us? We could provide short video segments, so by the time they get to their destination, it's not the first time they've looked at it. We have our videographers going out and taping a lot of the things that customers have questions about. We might have a video that says, "Here's what Rome Termini station looks like, this is where it is on the board, you just have to go right through here, and here's where you'll meet your train."

And then by the time they get there, they have an "Ah ha!" moment of recognition, and it all goes easily for them. Now, at what point do we send this information to them as a contact of content? Is it too much all at once? Is it sent out early on or up front? Well, let's ask them. When do they want to receive all this? We need to constantly think and rethink how often and what content we're sending to them.

We're constantly expanding this content and trying to add to it every time we go to new places. We add short videos, short instructional clips, different material for each country, even each station. It's going to be an archive of information, depending on what the customer needs.

We're building that up now. We've got videographers on staff, who will go on a certain number of trips. They're editing things together all the time, but we're arranging it so that we can visually tell the story in snippets. Again, we're not the owner of the product, we're an aggregator of thousands of services, that are complicated to put together, so our goal is to make it as smooth and easy for our travel agent partners to book and our customers to enjoy. Our goal is to provide world-class service throughout the experience.

Providing our customers with video guides is a relatively new add-on to our services. We make longer videos and then cut up certain segments. We'll use these segments in our proactive marketing, just little bits of each to give people a taste. But then, after people do put down their deposit and buy from us, we'll send them longer versions of these videos, specifically tailored to their trip.

We continue to build up the library of these video experiences to make it easier for our customers to navigate on their trip and bring their trip not only to life but to become familiar with the itinerary at the same time. These videos can be anything from what the journey is like from the train station to their chosen destination, to what the station looks like and how to get around it.

Some of the larger train stations in Europe can be quite confusing, especially if the signage is in a language you don't understand. And on that note, we also offer videos that have links back to how, for example, to read a Swiss train ticket (or whatever country they might be in). If they can read the train ticket, they can feel more confident and know what to present and where to go. We're constantly adding to the story with these videos, one that not only makes the journey easier, but also adds a bit of information and fun into the experience. It's an ongoing process for us as we refine the practice to make the whole experience easy for our customers.

We like to challenge ourselves with the idea that this particular practice is what we do or what we'd like to do, so let's take something that's complex and make it easier to understand. Rail travel can seem complex and confusing to people, especially if a customer is traveling to multiple cities or even multiple countries by train.

To help ourselves, we examine other companies that also have complex operations, and we look at what they do to simplify their information and put customers at ease. Going back to the RV example, we study what they did and see how well it's worked. We'll even look at other industries, such as insurance, to see how those companies might try to explain complicated products, services, and confusing policies to see how they present this information in an easy-to-understand way. And then we ask, "Can we use that format? Is there something there that we can apply to our own products and services?" We never want to stop learning.

MARKETING

FROM A MARKETING STANDPOINT, we also, as you might expect by now, focus on the customer. Everything that we do—who the customer is, what they want, the series of questions—all bleeds right into marketing. At the end of the day, our products can be anything a customer or travel advisor wants them to be, because everything is tailor-made and customizable, and that's how we create our rail packages. But to go up the funnel to see how that comes about, how they come to our products and services, we're also capturing customer information.

As an example, we have eleven different websites (we are in multiple countries with our brands), we send out lots of emails, and we do consumer and travel advisor webinars. We've been doing webinars for over ten years (we like to say "before it was cool"). We capture all that information, and we use it even when someone registers for a webinar. We again ask them questions in sets of three when they register for a webinar. For example:

- What are the three things you're looking to learn most in this webinar?

- What are the three reasons you are considering traveling by train to "x" destination?

- What are your top three questions you are looking for answers to about train travel?

We crunch all of the data from the answers to our questions and we serve that back up in marketing blogs, the subject lines of our emails, in content creation, and in short vignette videos explaining what we know customers will have questions about.

As an example, we'll produce guides asking questions like: "Want to know what it's like to travel by train? Click on this downloadable guide." It's a constantly evolving process, because it's related to product in many ways. People will have a question on a certain product or destination, such as, "Can you take the train around Ireland?" or "What's it like on the Venice Simplon-Orient-Express?" And we have the answer: "Here's a downloadable guide that will walk you through what you need to know."

But of course, we're not Google or Wikipedia. We like to say, "Our goal is to Tarantino it." Taking a page from director Quentin Tarantino who in many of his movies, starts with the end, and then works backward. We ask ourselves, what's the end result that we want? This is the exact result we want from a customer or a reseller.

We're relentless in making sure we market to the right customer. Period. Many times, we get asked, whether from our vendors, our resellers, or even our own staff: "Why don't we go after Gen Z?" or "Let's go after Millennials." They want to expand the market, and that seems like a good idea, but as we've said, when we look at who buys, they're a very specific target. It's the over-fifty customer who has the time and the money. Time is the big consideration, because outside of Europe, trains might not be so fast, and they might take longer from destination to destination, and if someone doesn't have that much vacation time, the train might not be their best option.

Although we'd love to expand the market to appeal to every single person, the reality is that this just isn't possible; the reality is that they aren't buying it. I personally see many companies that don't pay attention to who buys their products or services on a regular basis. If you want to know who your best customers are, you need go on the train and actually see who they are. Talk to them, find out what they're doing and why they are there.

One of the things we are most interested in is when a customer or travel advisor finds our product on their own or organically and it has nothing to do with our marketing or sales activities. This may sound counterproductive, like we're not measuring our marketing, but it's really about how they found us or want to use our products and services; we didn't market to them, they found us. These are the true diamonds, as they tend to have different reasons for why they are booking with us. If we ask the question and listen to why, we've just found another marketing message, a talking point; there are always more future customers who have the same questions about what they're looking for.

Now, we might want to add another category of customer, but the reality is that we have to appeal to them. We'll ask ourselves, "Why aren't we appealing to that category now? Is it too broad, is the trip too expensive for them, what is it?"

Also, what types of marketing do we have to use? Is it internet, blogs, or magazine articles? How do we reach those people? Ages fifty to seventy is a pretty big swath of people. They're probably looking at a variety of sources; different groups are going to be looking at different sources of travel information. Maybe someone who's seventy years old reads a magazine instead of going online. How are they finding us? What's the way that they're coming to us?

The answer is simpler than it might seem. Most of them find us because we're an answer to their question, a problem, or their unmet need. They might be Googling us, they might be looking on social media, or asking a friend; they're often online. They're looking for an answer on how to plan a successful trip, and we solve a problem for them. Many of them simply say, "I don't want to drive from here to here, I don't want to fly that distance. How would I do it by train?"

We create a lot of content; blogs, articles, vignettes, and videos, all explaining how to do many of these things directly, or through our reseller partners. We have the infrastructure in place now that many of them are simply finding us, because we offer something unique.

The other important component is that our traveler, whether they are fifty, seventy, or whatever age, they're still a traveler. There's still a bit of adventure in them, because if they really needed their hand held one hundred percent of the time, they would go on an escorted tour with a guide and be looked after the whole time, but that's not who our customer is. They might actually do an escorted tour pre- or post-main trip, they might do a cruise or river cruise pre- or post-main trip, but they're still self-sufficient in that they can handle things on their own. They might have questions, they might be a little nervous, but we put things out there to answer those questions or problems, and set their minds at ease from the start.

Here are some examples: How do they pack for the train? That might be a concern, if they've never traveled this way before. Or, what will the train connection time be for their transfer in Germany? We'll answer that.

Still, our customers are usually naturally adventurous when traveling, precisely because they're not going on a structured tour, with someone taking them the whole guided way. We try to appeal to that adventurousness, but make it simple, comfortable, and easy for them. We try to put that ease into marketing in various ways.

We like to include a "fun fact," or a "did you know?" We created a whole series of these: "Do you know how many train stations are in Europe?" and "Did you know that you can go from here to there?" Then we test out a lot of these ideas. Many of them are for our amazing travel advisors who resell our products to their customers, but many are also for customers: "Did you know that you can go to many of the American National Parks by train?" And they might reply: "Really? I didn't know you could do that."

As we've noted, we don't own anything. We aggregate thousands of products and services based on data and trends we see from what customers are quoting and buying.

A lot of the time, when you see marketing, what people are marketing is typically what's not selling for them. This might seem counterintuitive, but it's true. They're actually selling what they can't get rid of. It might be remnant space or it's just the higher margin stuff, but it's typically a lot of things that might not sell as easily.

For us, the only thing we put out there and market is what's working with our marketing, because nothing else matters to us. We don't have minimum numbers; it could be one person, or two people on different dates. Whatever we put out there is a trend happening as we're doing it, because we also want to be in the moment. We like to say that we like to catch the wave before it comes, not after it goes by. We never have to say, "Oh! I wish we'd had the product at that time."

This approach makes our marketing and sales changeable as trends change; we can keep up with new trends right in the moment, meaning we operate in real-time trends. We don't have to play catch up constantly.

This is also true for our websites. Our web team is very much in the loop with this practice. We'll say to them: "It's like we run a supermarket. At the end of the day, what do you want to put at eye level and up front?" And they're constantly rearranging the supermarket based on what's trending and happening at that moment, whether it's our UK, US, or Canadian site. Each of these sites have different products at different levels, different "shelves" in the supermarket, because one thing might be popular in the Australian market but not in the UK market, or vice versa. Luckily, we've got that fine-tuned machine working on it. We need to appeal to different people in different locations.

Again, it comes back to our central position: Are you really paying attention to the customer? What someone books this week might be very different from what people were booking last week, for whatever reasons. We have to keep up with that and find out why.

It's also worth noting that the customer is the same customer, whether they come to us direct or whether they go through a travel agent. The difference is that our messaging to a customer is very different than to a reseller, who might attract customers in a different manner.

But there's a level of passion, a level of excitement, a level of understanding about the journey, because they're the actual traveler. And at the end of the day, they're spending their own hard-earned money for this rail vacation. They may have been planning it for their whole life, and we take that very seriously. Someone could have been saving for thirty years for this trip, so we have nail it.

On the flip side, concerning our travel advisors who resell our products, we're exactly what we represent to them, that is, we make their jobs easier. They may not be as familiar with our products, the rail routes, or how it works, or maybe we're just a component of the overall trip they're putting together for their customers. Therefore, we offer them a subject matter expert (SME) who can give them the tools on a product that they may not be as familiar with, and/or connect the dots. We know the best way, the fastest way, and the best route. They don't have to be fearful of something that they're not as familiar with. We like to say that we give them back their time. They're not spending time online searching for everything they need. They'll call us, and this is what our focus and our specialty is.

A lot of people, friends or family, will ask me all kinds of different travel questions, and I say, "I can't really tell you about that." They'll always say the same thing to me: "But Frank, you're in the travel business, you've been in it for thirty years. How do you not know about it?" And I say, "I'll give you a great analogy. Think of me as a podiatrist and you're asking me a brain question. I work on your feet. I have no idea what's happening upstairs." And then they understand!

We focus on train travel, and stick with it, and then we partner with people who know about the other things. It saves travel agents time if they can plug right into our service, almost like a turnkey; they can just walk right in and there it is, and they don't have to do all the research on, for example, changing trains in Munich, and then going on to another destination; we already have all that information available.

Here is another example about our marketing strategies: My brother Jim is our head of sales, and a while ago, he had gone over to Switzerland. He had read some comments from a lot of our travel agent resellers and the questions that they had. When he was over there, he was with a couple of our staff members on a trip. He gave his phone to one member of the team and said, "Hey, just tape me." He's really the face of our company. They taped him on the train, he walked off the train narrating to the camera the whole time, and walked from the train station right into town, right to the hotel. He walked right here, and he did that little piece for travel agents. As we mentioned, that little snippet went viral.

Then as I went to different shows and I saw travel agents, and they said, "Oh my God, we loved your brother's video, we know that town! We know that town very well, but we know it from driving in or taking a bus in. We had no idea that the train station to the hotel was literally from here to there, versus having to drive in; it just came right in."

It opened up their minds, even among the agents that know that area very well. The difference is that they didn't know it from the train perspective, and what an easy way to travel it is. Many of these agents said, "We sent that to our customers, who were skeptical." They wanted to know how it was going to work taking the train, and the agents showed them: "Here's Jim, he just did it!" "Oh, it's that close?" "That's nothing!"

It's kind of surprising that with the rail network being so extensive and widely used in Europe that more people don't know about the ease of using it. One of the reasons for this is that for a lot of the travel industry (who are awesome), rail travel is still new to them. If you ask them about a cruise, they could tell you about every cruise ship, because that may be the volume, what they are booking a lot of. They book a lot of trips. We could just be a component, so they might not be as familiar with train options.

Their memory could be, "Oh, when I backpacked when I was twenty, I remember this..." So, what we're experiencing is with that "younger" generation. We say "younger" even though we're referring to the over-fifty customers again!

With our marketing, we're always exploring any way that we can have a new experience; we're always learning. How can we have a dialogue and not a monologue in any tactic and marketing? A monologue is great, but a dialogue is where the learning comes from. We're always exploring different tactics besides a click-download, follow path. Even outside of a webinar, we want to capture information. What other tactics can we use to get constant feedback?

Sure, we do surveys, but even then, we ask different questions on our website to try to help our customers narrow down what they like, in order to help give suggestions for places they have not even thought about yet. We capture that information, because we're trying to understand that customer, and work on how we can have a dialogue versus a monologue with them, because sometimes our perceptions are wrong. We want that new information "in our ear" all the time.

Another aspect of our marketing that we focus a lot of time on is the big difference between a shopper and a buyer in our line of business. There are a lot of people who will shop, the "lookies versus bookies" as we like to call them, because a lot of people might think, "Oh, that'd be great," but logistically it may not work for them. Someone might say, "I'm going golfing after, and I have to carry my clubs and gear on the train, and that doesn't work."

We always have to examine just who we're marketing to, and having a conversation with. We're comparing those kinds of objections to who actually books to be sure of what steps we need to take to get a customer from a "lookie" to a "bookie," or to determine if they might not actually be right for our product. They might be interested in train travel in general, but we may not be a fit for what they're looking for.

We're not going to convert every hit into a sale, and that's okay.

We never come up with anything on our own, and we never really need to. But then we ask ourselves, why would we "go fishing in a new pond" when we already have the "fish" that we need? Why approach new demographics? A lot of companies try to open up new markets and go into new demographics that maybe aren't so travel focused, and they try to appeal to demographics that really aren't their main customer base. We prefer to focus on what's already working. We remain very dedicated to our existing customer base, and we joke that we can almost nail them down to their blood type! We know what they like to do, why they're travelling, who's traveling together, how many people are in a group, what their age range is, and so on. All of this information is important to us if we're going to give them the best service possible.

These are the key points that we use in all of our marketing, whether in our email subject lines, or what we're putting where in an email, and even the font size and the imagery that we use. This is true for both email and on the website, as well. Everything is tailored to what those customers want to see. We don't, for example, put hiking in the Grand Canyon as an excursion for elderly travelers! There is always a temptation to say, "But this (whatever it might be) is so cool! Why not just include it in the package as an option?" But we don't want to lose focus, and all it would take is one email that's wrong in that way to turn off people, and have them say, "This isn't for me." And then, we've lost a potential customer.

This is a huge piece of our overall marketing. We do anything and everything we can to appeal to our chosen demographics. We work with a ton of travel agencies, which is another whole side of our marketing strategy. We educate them on what they need to share with their customers in those age ranges, to show them that our services are what can best help them.

When it comes to gathering marketing information, we've found that post-booking, pre-travel surveys are the most important to us. Most companies focus on post-travel surveys only: "Tell us how your trip went." But we prefer the post-deposit, pre-departure survey, long before the trip has even begun. It's very helpful for us when creating our different marketing campaigns. We can learn how they heard about us, what are their main questions, and ask them the "top three" questions. We analyze those answers frequently. A whole team serves that data up to our marketing team in a very visually easy-to-consume way. We find, as we've mentioned, that many of our customers want to take a pre- or post-cruise with the rail trip; it's an extremely popular add-on. But we want to go beyond that and know why they're traveling, not only on the trip itself, but why with us specifically.

For our website, we did a complete consumer analysis: where people are clicking, what pages they're visiting most often, etc., and we designed the whole site based on those studies. How are our customers getting from the top of the funnel to the bottom, that is, from the initial state of being interested to making a booking? And how can we make that process easy for them?

We needed to understand how different customers search for things, because it will be different for different people. Are they coming in with certain wants or needs? If so, could they have those more easily with our help? If they don't have a clear sense of what they want, can we suggest a package for them? Or if they know exactly what they want and where they want to go, can we accommodate that?

We have to make using our website easy. One thing we offer is that people can search on our site by map. We've always known that customers love searching by maps, and we realized that we needed to provide that. We have made all kinds of maps downloadable on our site (train routes, for example) in addition to fliers and other information that customers can access before or during their trip. Downloading is a call to action for the customers that they enjoy doing, and that information is added to a customer's profile. Customers have told us that they often have no idea about the train network (especially in the US), where a train goes, and so on. And most people have no idea, no real concept of what rail networks look like.

We tend to appeal to a general audience with moderate activities, rather than going for extremes, which again, draws certain types of customers to us. You won't likely find bungee jumping and extreme sports in our packages! We do offer things like bike tours and such for those who want to do them, but they are most often not the main focus.

A big part of our marketing relies on our analysts and the information they send us. The number of customer data point reports we receive from our analytics team is almost overwhelming, but it's fantastic! They're really guiding us, telling us where to go based on the information we're getting. And this is why we don't have to come up with everything ourselves, or decide what to do with marketing. The customers are literally telling us what to do, and giving us the "whys" of what they want from us. We get new information multiple times a week, so it's really never-ending. We can just get on with our work, which involves taking that information and working with it.

We will launch new products based on customer demand, but when we do it, we need a clear sense of why we're doing it, and what customers are asking for. We look at their top answers and make those our focus for emails, webinars, and so on; we don't need to come up with it on our own. We could try to be fun and trendy and push some new destination that no one is asking about, but why should we? Instead, we push what we know people are booking. It seems so simple, but it works!

As for the "breadcrumbs" for people to get to us and our website, we work with a lot of travel agents who refer their customers to us. We are offering a service that not many others do or are even able to offer. Agents are eager to work with us because we fill an important niche that they need. It's a kind of word-of-mouth marketing that is invaluable.

We also offer blogs. We're putting out about three blogs a week on average, and we've found that they are really useful for people and helpful for us. We use the "top five" or "top ten" list format for many of our blogs, and it's a format that continues to be popular. People enjoy reading lists, which is why we incorporate them into so much of what we do.

Indeed, one of our best blogs is one called "5 of the Best Scenic Rail Journeys in Switzerland." Amazingly, we actually get more traffic to that page than we do to our home page, because of the amount of web searches coming from people who are looking for just that kind of information. It comes up organically in web searches, and our SEO is well-tailored to be at the top when people look on Google, or wherever they might be searching. So, they read the blog, and click right on through to us for more information.

We're fortunate in that we've been established for a long time now, which gives us a larger presence online, without having to work extra hard just to be seen. Web searches will often lead back to us and our services.

But we're not resting on our laurels. One of our more innovative marketing ideas has been in partnering with game shows, and we've been involved with *Wheel of Fortune* for some time. Offering up a full rail package as one of the grand prizes has been great for us. Older viewers tend to like such shows, which skews right into our main demographic. And we know it works, because when we ask about how customers have heard about us, *Wheel of Fortune* frequently comes up, especially in the days after one of our trips is offered on the show. Sometimes, it works a bit too well: once, we had so many inquiries the day after a prize was offered on the show that our website crashed! Not the best outcome for our web tech people, but honestly, we'll take it!

You will also see us on *The Price is Right*, and we look forward to working with them going forward. We're adding more marketing like this all the time, and we can't wait to see where it goes. We've not done a lot of direct consumer marketing, but these shows offer us new and easy ways to reach others in our target market. It's like they were made for us!

We will also take initiative on our own to get the word out. We do flash sales from time to time, which can be huge for us. These are usually sales that are on offer for only a week or so, which can create a sense of urgency and demand. For us, they can be great for boosting revenue, or achieving a sales goal. And for the customer, they get a great deal and the satisfaction of getting something that was not widely on offer; it's almost like winning a prize on a game show! It's great marketing all on its own. If someone feels they're getting a great deal, they'll be more likely to spread the word, which is additional advertising for us.

We're also doing more press work to get out the word. One of the packages we've put together is called "Around the World by Luxury Train." We've done it in years past, but now, we're focusing on the luxury aspect much more, and want to market it extensively. It costs $200,000 per person, and it's on all of the major luxury rail lines around the world. Of course, given the cost, it's not going to have a huge number of bookings, but it makes a great story, and we can get tons of press for it. Offering up a story about modern luxury travel is both a product push and a marketing push at the same time, while also being a fun way to get our name out there and educate the public in what we do. It shows readers who we are and where we go, and we make it easy for them to book a portion of the package, instead of the whole thing. Just a small amount of luxury!

Luxury travel has its very specific market, of course, and we position ourselves as experts in it, as well as around-the-world rail travel. It's a niche within a niche, and sometimes being more specific is the right way to go. People can choose to buy the whole package or just a portion, but either way, they'll be getting a unique experience, backed by top-notch service that ensures that their trip will be memorable.

WHOEVER ASKS THE MOST QUESTIONS, WINS

GETTING BACK TO OUR THEME about "staying on track" and seeing things through the customer's eyes on a regular basis, we again ask them and ourselves what those top three things are that are the most important to them.

I started thinking about what are the things that we do on a regular basis, or that someone else could do in their line of business, to make sure that customer focus is the prime goal. We are always "secret shopping"; we do that ourselves. We have some of our management team send fake emails, and we email in like a customer. We also actually have an outside company that we pay that "secret shops" us on a regular basis, because we constantly want to see and hear things through the customer's eyes.

We do this because we don't always know when something on the website hasn't been updated properly, or it's the wrong information, or someone didn't get back to a customer in a timely manner. This kind of checking is really easy to do; it takes a little discipline but we learn every time. We'll make a fake booking, we'll have someone come in as a customer, we'll send fake emails, we'll send a request for more information, and so on. It's easy enough to do and you learn every time, because it's always a little bit different than what you think it might be. For example, how did that content get there specifically? Why are we saying a given thing? Why was the response so slow, and why didn't it get there at the correct time?

We also examine other companies to measure ourselves against them. We want to see, for example, how quickly do they respond, what are they putting in their content, and other such details. Even if they're not a travel company, we try to look at best practices just to get a sense of their operations, and how we measure up. We want to know who provides services, the best kind of information, and even if it's a totally different company, how can we incorporate their successes into our model. This might be in our training, our education, or our technology; there's always something we can learn from others.

We always ask our customers and the travel agents that do book with us why they're using us; what service do we provide that makes us stand out? We take in that information and tweak what's working to make it better. People like that we solve problems (even before they come up), that we make the process easy for them, and that they don't have to do as much research on their own.

We take this kind of feedback and consider it in how we structure the company, what roles we each have in it, and how to best integrate new ideas. We get together every September and talk about what has worked what hasn't in the previous year, but we'll be implementing new ideas and discussing them all year round.

We explore what roles we should have but currently don't. We want to see if there are kinks in the hose anywhere along the customer journey and respond to those. That often means that we have to create new roles. However, sometimes a role doesn't have to exist anymore and we no longer need it, because some form of automation has come in. We want to focus on speed, simplicity, and scalability. How can we go faster, how do we make it easier, and how can we scale it versus something that's non-scalable?

Data is just one point of the process. At the end of the day, we must listen to the customer, otherwise our company is just not going to work. Without customers, we don't have paychecks, and we're out of business. It really is that simple. We can talk about leadership, but ultimately, we're also "servants" to the customers.

In travel, a lot can always go wrong, so being sympathetic to that uncertainty is a huge part of our work. The world isn't perfect, especially not when it comes to travel. There are going to be delays, cancelations, changes in plans, and so on, so our success comes down to how we validate the customer and handle these issues as they come up. It might be a problem that we have no control over at all: a flight delay, lost luggage, bad weather, etc. We just have to make sure that a customer always feels valued and that we listen to them.

Again, we always remind ourselves that someone might have saved money their entire life for this trip. They could be retired and on a limited income, or maybe they just don't have a lot of money, or come from means. So, this trip might be the once-in-a-lifetime vacation that they'll always remember, the bucket list trip that they've always wanted to do. We tell ourselves, "This could be my grandmother. She has this one thing she's always wanted to do, and she's trusting us to get it right." With that in mind:

- How can we do better?
- How can we perform better?
- How can we serve our customers better?
- How can we? That's the question.

If we don't ask these questions, we're shutting our minds off to new possibilities and answers.

We set aside the idea of impossible and ask, "But what if we could?" By doing that, we start thinking differently and collaborating differently. All of a sudden, we find ourselves in new places we never even thought we could get to. Why not try this new idea? Can we? Why not? Do we have any data to support the idea? If so, can we actually do it?

We run models for new ideas and ask what it will cost us, in time, effort, and in money. Even if it doesn't work out, what are we going to learn by doing it? For example, are we going to include a new experience like a secret food tour or a new add-on destination, theme, or city combination based on interest? The learning is in the doing and that's where we can often find real value. Even if the idea doesn't work out like we want, we look for what we can learn from it. Let's say that an idea costs us $20,000, but that idea doesn't work. We don't curse, get angry, and feel sorry for ourselves. Instead, the next step is to ask, "How can we get $20,000 worth of learning out of it?" We'll look at the idea again and how we might approach it differently, so that we can build on it. The failed idea was just the first step, and that's where we can really shine.

All of us love to learn, and the best learning can sometimes come from the mistakes. We evolve ourselves and our staff in the process as we learn and grow. The organization has to be adaptable to constant change. We all have to. The external environment is always changing, even if we don't like it. Removing oneself from one's comfort zone is essential in a business like ours; if you don't adapt, you're out of business. Disruptions are inevitable, and you have to get ahead of them.

We'll get the resources, we'll make the process more efficient, we'll add another employee … whatever it takes if we get more customer satisfaction. As long as we take care of the customers, everything else flows: the money, the work, the success.

We're in the service business, not unlike a restaurant. We have customers coming in, ordering specific things off of a "menu," and expecting great service.

Ultimately, every problem is an opportunity for change and growth. Every problem can be figured out in some way. It might not always be obvious. It might not be the way we wanted to solve it, but we remain open to changes and new solutions, which has served us very well over the years. We have no doubt that we'll continue doing so well into the future.

FOCUS AND DISCIPLINE

SOMETIMES I'LL SAY TO OUR TEAM: "What stands out to you when you're explaining a point?" I like that question because it helps us learn and understand what others are talking about.

I'm reminded of Caroll Spinney, who used to play Big Bird on Sesame Street. He wrote the book *The Wisdom of Big Bird, Lessons in Life and Feathers*. One of the things I use with my team is the "Big Bird Rule." He talked about how his first couple of years in the 1960s playing Big Bird, he couldn't really see out of the costume, and as the puppeteer, he tripped over stuff. He had a hard time, and back then, they actually created what was almost like a monitor in the Big Bird puppet so that he could see. He talked about how he had to do that for thirty years, and how it made him a better actor, a better puppeteer.

The whole point of the story is that he saw from camera 1's angle, camera 2's angle, camera 3's angle. He could only see what he looked like to the audience. I use that a lot with our staff to say, "Let's make sure we all follow the Big Bird Rule: we need to look at the situation through cameras 1, 2, and 3, just like Caroll did." He saw his whole career, he looked through the audience's eyes, the customers' eyes.

We talk about that a lot in our meetings, where I like to remind everyone about the rule. How does this situation look to our travel advisors, our customers, our prospects? I reference this idea regularly and it's something that, once I go over it with our team, it really stays with them. They talk about it in meetings, and we make sure we stick with the Big Bird Rule.

It's easy to drift away from it, so we always need to redirect our focus.

We talk about "World-Class" service and of always challenging ourselves to make sure to provide it, not only to customers, but also to our travel advisors. That's an ongoing effort and it's never-ending because things change so much in this industry. What's important to someone on a service level changes, partly because technology changes, and we have to stay on top of that. But we also have to be mindful of what's important to someone at the right time, so I use this example (and this is going to be a funny one!): when I turned fifty, my doctor said, "Congratulations, you have to get a colonoscopy!"

I thought, "Great, that's fantastic." But I'm a baby with needles, I hate needles. And this is true for a lot of people, so obviously, who's going to say, "Yes, I can't wait!"

I'll be honest, I was nervous. I had to go there, but from the time I had the video orientation with the doctor, the relationship was fantastic. He was a great guy and made me feel at ease. And it was even better: the first person I met at the counter welcomed me and congratulated me for getting the exam done, and even thanked me for being there. They asked if I needed anything, and again really made me feel welcome and relaxed.

The anesthesiologist came over, a big gentleman from Nigeria. I'd mentioned that I'm nervous about needles, so he puts his hand on my shoulder and says, "I got you, my friend."

The other nurses gave me the needle, and told me not to worry. There was a tremendous amount of kindness, from the rolling in and waiting for the doctor, to the other nurses talking to me, and telling me not to worry. The doctor comes in, 3-2-1, here comes the stuff, bang!

I wake up after, and the doctor said, "Hey, you did great!"

Everyone I interacted with was wonderful, even the nursing student taking me out to the car, and saying, "Thank you so much."

I get home and they gave me the results—and I'm not making this up—I have a handwritten thank-you note from the colonoscopy clinic!

I use this funny story as an example for my team. I say, "How do you take something that someone's not excited about, maybe fearful about, especially if they're scared of needles, and make it good? How does a colonoscopy turn into world-class service?"

I even asked the head nurse on the way up: "How many of these do you do a day?"

"Oh," she said, "up to eighty a day."

Eighty! How do you give that kind of personalized, kind, easy service to every single person and include a hand-written thank-you note? It's incredible! I've since reached out to the head of Mission Hospital just to compliment them.

So, in the day-to-day, you're in the travel business, doing something that's fun and exciting, but you can't take it for granted that you're giving world-class service. Let's be honest, if someone can turn a colonoscopy into world-class service, then maybe we should push even more with what we're trying to do, and not just be casual or not care so much. And for the record, my team always says, "The colonoscopy story is awesome!"

TECHNOLOGY

THE ONE THING ABOUT TECHNOLOGY and staying on track is that tech is evolving all the time, whether it's a vendor, a customer, a travel advisor, or an operator. We're all trying to stay ahead of technology, whether we love it or not. It's more about making sure that we have the right technology and making sure that the customer, advisor, or vendor wants to interact with us on a regular basis, as well as how they absorb or get information or go back and forth.

It's a constantly evolving thing, and for us as a company, it's changing all the time. We want to stay ahead of it, of course, but a lot of our task is making sure that it's easy for people to jump on a technology that is what I call the "new shiny penny." Maybe it hasn't been adopted by everyone yet, so some people want to be the first, or at least they think they do. But does it really make a difference?

I say that because again, you must always ask what kinds of technology do your customers want to interact with on a regular basis? Maybe that new tech is slowly being adopted, so you don't want to be late to the party, of course. But really, what's important to your customer and how are they interacting with it? I think too many times—and I do see this sometimes with travel advisors, vendors, and partners—they want to be the first with a given new technology, but it hasn't been widely adopted yet, and sometimes it's never adopted from a customer base. Still, you'd like to have it, but you can't go all in on a new technology if there's not an adoption; you need to keep that dialogue going with those customers.

I am a big believer that new technology should make things easier for the customer first and the company second. Too many times, I see technology rolled out that makes things more efficient for the company—where they don't need as many staff since the technology handles the function—but is confusing and more work for the customer. Think of how often we call a company for service and soon, we're seven levels deep into a call tree that keeps asking us questions to get to the right person and we just want to yell: "Operator, help!"

Whether our customers want to chat online, want to text in, want "an app for that," our goal is to provide whatever way they want to interact with us, so we can support it and give good service. In some cases, we strategically decide to slow down certain technologies to fully embrace, understand them, and ensure they are easy for our customers.

So, whether it's a travel advisor, consumer, or vendor, are you always looking not only at new technology and testing new technology, but also asking of your customer and travel agent base what they want to get into? Because too many kinds of tech come in and out.

Years ago, everyone thought that a travel podcast would be the biggest thing. Now, are podcasts big? Sure, they are. But are they big in travel? Not really. Is video big? Sure, it is.

Online chat? Online chat goes in and out. Is it going to be bigger in the future? Probably. Is email important? It is but it's becoming less important. Things are already cluttered, so how do people sift through the clutter?

My point is that new technology is a never-ending journey to where we need to be, but we also need to understand it and always consider if it's really being adopted. And if so, how do we enhance it and make it easier? Also, if it's not being adopted, why? We will never force new technologies on our customers or travel advisors.

We ask them: how do you get information? How much do you get on your mobile phone? Is it email? Is it text? Is it research? Is it websites? How do you want to get information, whether you have pre-travel info, grabbing information, thinking about it, researching it, and so on.

Are you in the secondary phase of researching and now you're getting into details of depositing prior to departure from the logistics of it? Technology is always evolving but it's never what you think it's going to be at times, because it's really about the adoption, and it's hard to always tell what will be adopted and what won't.

Often times, a company is looking at their own efficiency, again, not thinking about it from the customer's perspective. That doesn't mean you can't try to have it as an option, but if the customer's not adopting some new tech and they don't want it, or you don't have another means for them to communicate to get information, you're creating a barrier for them. Why create a barrier especially when it's something very pleasurable, like taking a vacation, something they're looking forward to? Why make it hard because you're trying to be efficient on your end?

Don't set things up just to be convenient for yourselves.

I'm a newspaper reader. I get the *New York Times*, the *L.A. Times*, the local Orange County paper, and the *Wall Street Journal*. I still like reading newspapers, and I read them all on Sunday. Someone asked me recently, "Why do you read all the papers on Sunday? You could just go online and Google information."

And I said, "The reason I read the Sunday papers is because *I like finding things I wasn't looking for*. When I Google, I find what I need for that specific topic, but I also like discovering things locally: hey, there's an art festival that I didn't know was happening. Or maybe I'm reading a story I would never have looked up because I didn't know enough about it. If I only search for what I'm looking up, I keep getting fed back only what I'm looking at, seeing a narrow view. But I want to see what else is going on and learn, versus just constantly being fed."

Recently, my wife went to the supermarket. She was going to a baby shower and bought diapers for one of her clients. Well, the coupons at the supermarket then gave her baby formula discounts for herself! So, if you automate so much, you forget who that customer is.

You see this everywhere: everything you click on immediately assumes you want more of the same. You click on a YouTube video, and then it suggests more examples, but maybe I don't need three other suggestions. Everything is set up like this now, and it feels like it's completely lost the human touch. Everything is just computers running in the background, feeding you what they assume you want based on what you've clicked. Targeted ads are based on these algorithms now. Everyone gripes about Facebook and everyone else doing this stuff, but it's happening everywhere, all the time.

Tying this annoyance back to technology, we always want to ensure that technology is not just sending our customers what we think they'll like. We want it to be personal. We might even throw in something new, something as a surprise: a different destination, a different product, a different service that they may not have thought about previously. This is far better than just feeding information into a computer, like the diapers or social media recommendations. We want to offer customers something different, maybe a destination that they wouldn't have even thought of and give them a reason as to why they might want to go there.

We want to offer everyone a little extra. If we see an over-all trend for a destination, we might recommend it, even if that customer's not looking for that specific place, because it's just expanding their minds a little. We're showing them where else the train goes, maybe some place that they might not know about, which is pretty cool.

We want to be sure that what we're putting out there is not only popular and trending; we also put out what's new and when we do, we start to see—even if the volume's not there at first—travelers who say things like, "Oh, I didn't know you could do that by train, that looks interesting!" Whether it's an off the beaten path destination or a bigger place. These personalized touches make a difference.

We don't want technology to run away with things and take over. We still need the human touch, and we always put that in. It's not just about turning on the machine and letting it run.

Another big problem is that you can get lost with so many different technologies and communication channels. You're adding new elements in constantly, and all of the sudden, you don't have a single system, you have multiple systems. Is it just me, or is the amount of communication and technology overwhelming and difficult to respond quickly enough to? I counted the other day in a one-hour period of time: I had over *700* messages to myself from nine different sources (email-work, email-personal, LinkedIn, Facebook, Instagram, X, WhatsApp, text, and Teams Chat); these came from customers, travel advisors, vendors, and staff. Many people put in multiple sources to ensure I received their message. Where to begin? Responding can be a problem. Imagine the how the customer feels!

Getting back to the customers, look at how many different websites you sometimes have to visit to find a product or service for travel: potential customers or travel advisors go to the rail company site, the hotel site, the destination site, and so on. And how many different sites do you go to either to operate your business, or sell a package? Customers might search for a long time only to find that's just not the right product or service, which can be frustrating.

Our business is about answering the right questions people might have, which might be secondary in some cases to the destination. So, we're starting to move them down a path where people are asking things like: "Hey, where can we go last minute? Where can we go that has this feature we want? Well, I never thought about that, outside of Rome, Florence, and Venice, what else can we do there, what else is popular? What else is a great activity?"

It's crucial to make sure that you use technology to enhance that customer's research process, not just to feed them what you think they want. This is a big concern for us, and it's a work in progress. We're not perfect at it, but we're always trying.

What's interesting to me on the technology side is that no matter what technology comes into play and how many cool bells and whistles it might have, in the travel space, in the consumer space, it still always comes down to the same thing. Regardless of how you get there, someone's looking for an experience, someone's looking for a vacation, a holiday, where they travel by themselves, with friends, family, loved ones, etc. They want an amazing experience, and in many cases, maybe they don't have a lot of vacation time. They want to make sure that if they're spending their hard-earned money, they want to make it count, they want to have those memories of a lifetime.

Therefore, I never get too caught up in technology. I want to get caught up in the journey and the experience that we can provide, pre-travel. It's that research, looking into it, the excitement of it, that matters. Then you want to deliver that when it's time, and obviously, if and when they come back to travel again. Technology is just a component of the whole process, but too many times, you can get caught up in the idea that technology will just take care of it.

It's important to remember that travel is human. Travel is emotional, often very emotional for people, so you must make sure that the human element is always injected into the process. And that's how we look at technology, which is different, I think, than many other businesses.

It's amusing, because a lot of our technology has some "manualness" to it, as well. I keep it manual because sometimes that's where the learning is. I'll give an example of what I mean: even though I put it under "technology," in our company we have two things:

- A team of people dedicated solely to listening; focused on the phones. However, they don't listen to our account execs talking to our travel advisor consumer, they're not there to monitor our staff, we have our trainers that help them. Instead, they're there to listen to the emotion, the interaction, the questions that the travel advisors and customers are asking to make sure that we're delivering that information in whatever form they're looking for: web, email, webinar, etc.

- In a lot of our online forums, we always have an open field for comments, which our data teams don't like, because it's harder to measure. They'll say, "just have a drop-down, that's just the same thing." But how do you know that the drop-down contents are, for example, the things you're actually looking for? Our data teams hated it at first, but they've come to love it. The open field is where all the "diamonds" are. You'd be so surprised at how many times the travel advisor or even the consumer has a lot to say in an open field, and they will share their excitement, their passion, and their emotion in asking a question. And that's where you start to see comments like: it's their twenty-fifth anniversary, or wow, they did this when they were backpacking, or they can't wait to do this one thing. This information then gives us an opportunity to again deliver world-class service, to really exceed their expectations. That's what's important to them.

This is why we keep that "manualness" to our technology, and I tell our team, "No, we're the human technology, we're the manual technology."

Our work is still technology, because we're data sourcing, but in a way that is human. So, whether it's a travel advisor or reseller, we advise not to just let the machines do it.

Ask yourself: Are you listening? Are you paying attention? Because they'll give you those diamonds if you listen or look hard enough. If you're just using a drop-down field that comes in an Excel report, maybe you're missing some of the most valuable information. Don't just automate because you want things done quickly and efficiently; that can miss out on some really important information.

The company's convenience isn't as important as listening to genuine feedback. We all want to be more efficient, but if you use efficiency without paying attention, if you're too efficient, you'll never have the right product development or content development on what's important to people because you're always making assumptions. We have that ability to listen, learn, and to create opportunities for open fields.

We do aggregate all of that information—submitting in an open field, a ticket, and listening—which usually rounds out or takes us in a little bit of a different direction, because it contains information that can't be put into a drop-down. Without an open field for feedback, you can't feel the emotion in a transaction or the "why," and the why has much more of that.

Again, technology is a different word to us. It's not just "technology," it's bigger than that; it guides us too. I would ask any partner, vendor, looking at this issue:

- Are you seeing technology as efficiency?

Okay (I'm skeptical), but it's more than that. You don't have to be manual on everything, but you do have to touch on it once in a while, and you need to have a way that's still "in your ear."

The drop-down problem happens a lot in online help. Where they're asking you what the problem is, and you get a drop-down of like five options, but none of those are your problem! So, what do you do? That happens so often with software and websites; you go to their online help and you can't type in your problem, you have to choose one of the five or six pre-chosen options, and that's not helpful.

I had a recent experience with this problem. My Apple Watch just went off for some reason. I didn't want to go to the store, so I decided to just chat online, and it took me a while to finally get there, go here, go here, go there, etc. And the help took me through the automated portion, not the live chat. It just said, "Do this, look here, and look in this directory, and read through all the problems."

I finally got there, and I finally got to a live chat with some-one on the other side of the world, even with the delay. They were able to help me, but I remember thinking to myself, "I probably could have driven to the store in the same amount of time that it took me to dig through this, if not faster." Who is this website really helping? If it isn't faster to do that, then what's the point? It's supposed to be for convenience.

The other example that everybody hates is phone queues, where you have to keep pushing buttons before you can speak to a human being, you cycle through this to get to the operator that you wanted to speak to ten minutes before any-way, so how is that helping anyone? Then you get through to them and they ask you what your problem is again, so obvi-ously they didn't get that info that you typed in, so what was the point of doing any of it? That is when it hit me: when a company puts everything online and you do it all yourself, they don't work for you, you actually work for them. I am not saying that I'm not in favor of this and supportive of doing it online. I am, but does that fit every customer?

Even though most of our customers are fifty and over, we have ranges, we have customers that might not text, we have some that are all about texts, some that love phones, and others that hate them. How do you make it easy for everyone? You simply can't let technology be the sole way to do this. If someone is not an adopter of that particular technology, now they're stuck, and they'll probably take their business elsewhere.

Travel is an always-changing environment, meaning there's always a new destination, a new hot spot, because something gets seen in a movie or what have you. The cus-tomer dictates everything to us, but we also work to ensure that our internal processes and our internal structure continue to make it easy for a potential customer. This means that every year we're changing drastically.

I used to bring my leadership team together every September and we would review what worked this year, and what didn't. For the things that didn't work, we asked ourselves, "How could we make them work for next year?" Whether that's a process, a technology, or positions, or it could be all of those things, and then we look further at that every quarter, and ask, is that working? If not, we course-correct to make sure that everything is working for us.

A past example of this was that we once tried group departures but it didn't go with our model; we got rid them. But we saw an opportunity to create an innovation team where we could consistently be looking at new technology deriving from challenges and opportunities that we experienced, based on our growth. Cutting one and adding the other has helped us tremendously. Today, we don't wait until September; we have moved to changing in real time. How do we do that? As you can imagine, there is a lot of technology measuring all aspects of how a customer interacts with us on their journey, from concept to quote, to booking, to departure and return. We have many reports, automatic quality controls, and alerts. But to break them down simply, we meet as a full management and leadership team every Monday and review all key measurements. And we will adjust on the fly, shifting staff, departments, and focus to match our customers' and travel agents' needs, wants, concerns, and aspirations. Let's not forget that this is someone's vacation we are talking about as we deliver memories of a lifetime; we take it seriously.

In any changing environment, whether it's a small, medium, or a large business, you must make sure that you know what customers have to say at all times. Always keep them in your ear so you don't go off track, and if and when something happens, you actually know what to do, because the dialogue is already built into your business model on a regular basis.

It needs to be much more than, "Let's do a survey once a year and see what they think." That doesn't work, that's too late. I credit our company and all of our team and management, because they're skilled, attuned, and they already speak the customer language that's part of their DNA. It was difficult to pivot during the down time, but it wasn't as difficult as I saw for some of my friends and colleagues at other companies, where they froze. They didn't know what to do, because they didn't have that closeness and ongoing dialogue, and they didn't have that path of feedback all the time, beyond just a "once in a year" thing with their customers.

At the foundation is knowing who your customer is, why are they buying today, who are they, and for those that aren't buying, why are they not? I say pay attention to those who are buying, versus those who aren't, because those who are not, there's a billion reasons why not. It could be anything, especially in the travel business, because we're a want not a need. There are those that tell you why every day, if you listen. Even when things get bad, well, who's booking when it's bad? And how do you get more of them? Some people focus on the idea that they need to go more after this market or that segment ... okay, but you're not paying attention to those who are buying now. That doesn't mean you can't expand your market, but in a changing market, doing what we've done will take you to double the size in the most complex scenario, if you're paying attention.

It almost seems like a revolutionary idea, when it actually should be almost painfully obvious, but so few companies seem to be able to do this. You see it so often: they just kind of dig their heels in and stay with what has always worked for them. I think it's really interesting, the resistance that a lot of businesses throw up to these kinds of changes, even though they're often unavoidable.

I'm always amazed by it; it honestly really surprises me. I'm talking about great companies, too. I'm so surprised at how often they have a certain way of doing things, they dig their heels in, and they really don't—at least on an ongoing basis—pay attention to their customers. They say that they do, but actually, they just don't. I love asking the question of other companies: "Tell me, how do you keep in touch with your customers, can you show me right now, what's the feedback today? How do you know?"

Often, they have no good answer, and you can tell very quickly that they really don't know. When things are good, it's because everyone has a reason why things are good, but they could do more than that just by paying attention. When things aren't good, you can really start to see it because they freeze, but you can make your way through the tough times if you know more. It's that ongoing dialogue that makes changing environments easier to maintain. And again, it's made us who we are today.

Of course, some of this resistance might have to do with internal company pressures. If you're a publicly traded company and have investors and shareholders, they'll be more conservative about making radical changes, because they don't want to see the next quarter dip. Perhaps smaller companies have more freedom to take risks because of their nature. The bigger the company, the more publicly traded, the more investors, the less likely they are to change.

So, who's the master and who's the boss? Is it the shareholders, and they're less risk averse because they have investments? Probably. Is it a different entity versus a private company that's more entrepreneurial, because they have to be? Maybe there aren't investors covering that, for good and bad, so you don't have those funds, but you have to get the return somehow, so you take fewer risks.

Some companies go to a third party to do some research, and produce results. They'll say "Yeah we did analysis, this is where we should go."

And I say, "Okay, you did three case studies and you studied a segment, you brought a few people in, but can't you just listen to your customers every day? It's so easy!"

It might seem difficult to learn how to capture that, but look, if I can figure it out, anybody can figure it out; it's not that difficult! If you discipline yourself to listen, it's amazing.

I'll give another example: I have all of our management listen to calls one to two hours a week, every week, and after, they have to submit what they heard to one of our directors. That feedback gets reviewed every week. Now they're not listening so much for specifics, to that one person on the phone who didn't do something. Instead, they're listening to have a feel. What's the overall tone?

The results are amazing. You start to hear and see so much more. It's like going into a room in an art gallery and just sitting there, listening to what people have to say about the art. You can think whatever you want about it, whether you're the artist, or the gallery owner. But when you look at the customers who spent their time and money to be there, and especially if you listen to people who are buying that artwork, and you just observe and take notes, how does that help you in the next exhibition or art gallery? A lot!

That's how I like to look at things. I ask, are we doing this on a regular basis? Because once you start assuming, you know the saying: "ASS out of U and ME." I discipline myself and our team on that, and they're really good about it. Almost every week, I'll have one of them, one of our managers say something about it. One of the managers from the UK told me, "Oh my God, it's so good, I love the fact you have us do this, I learn these things, and no book is going to give you that."

We have the discipline to do that because it's live learning. It's real time and it's always changing. We feel that it's a great, even innovative policy. Thinking about it, it seems so obvious, almost absurdly so, and yet most companies don't do things like this, as I find every day in dealing with people in our industry and beyond.

COMPLEX VS. COMMODITY PRODUCTS

YOU HAVE TO CONSIDER COMPLEXITY versus commodity in your product or service no matter what product that is. Whatever you're selling or marketing—a product or a service—you always need to make sure that your business stays on the complex side and not the commodity side. This is because if the business is on the commodity side of our industry, then your service becomes all about price and people can do it themselves, or someone will offer it cheaper.

We position ourselves on the complex side, that is, we take care of all of the little details that a customer doesn't want to have to deal with. Customers need that level of support, especially if you intend to give them the best possible service. They would rather go with an expert rather than just trying to do it all themselves. When customers want five-star luxury at rock bottom prices with white-glove service, we ask them to pick two of those options!

We don't suffer from a lack of inventory. We're different than, say, a river cruise. At some point, that ship may sell out its cabins, and that ship may only allow for a maximum of 120 people on board. So, it doesn't matter if I want to travel on that specific day, that ship is sold out, too bad! The next ship might not go for another week, or when this one returns. You'll just have to wait.

That doesn't happen on the rail side. There are plenty of cars and carriages, or one's travel can wait one day, or go the next day, etc. This puts rail travel in an exciting space.

There's never a lack of customers that want to take the train, and there's not a lack of inventory to satisfy that need. And that fact creates a space where there's huge opportunity for growth. I look at other industries where they might be capped by who actually wants the service or how much they can provide. Those offerings can be very specific, and that's fine, that's a narrow market, but is it still complex versus commodity-based, or is it a market where it has very limited availability? Hopefully, your margins are higher.

Ask yourself, where are you in that business model and where is it going?

Your job is always to be in a space where you can stay in the complex and make it complex versus just commodity. Because when it's commodity, just price, and it's online, you risk getting eliminated. Not too long ago, I took a five-day, four-night trip across Canada. It was a straight-through trip; I wasn't disembarking anywhere. There are lots of questions I had that go with that kind of trip. I had to check my bag. I couldn't have a big bag in my room for five days and four nights, so where is it stored? Is there Wi-Fi or not? And is that all along the trip, or only at certain locations. How do meals work? How does everything work? Hey, where's the electrical plug in here? How do I charge my devices? What do I bring with me?

As you can see, there are a lot of a lot of questions that go with what seems like a simple enough trip. Can you lock your room? There are showers on board, but how do I use them? What are the water levels, since a train can't just carry endless amounts of water across a whole continent?

Indeed, water issues are a big deal, one of the things I didn't know anything about until I got on board. In my room, the "prestige class," we had a shower in the room. However, in other sleepers, there's a private, yet shared shower in the carriage for the group. Now, in the shower, there's a button, and every sixty seconds or so, you press the button or the water will shut off. This is because years ago, someone accidentally left the shower on for five hours and drained all the water out of the train! That was a painful lesson, to be sure.

You don't usually think of things like this until you're actually there, but it's a pretty basic question: how do I clean myself? This isn't the kind of thing that customers will usually get answered on the up-front portion of a travel booking, and that's where we come in, to make sure that all of the details are carefully explained to them, all the little things that never would have occurred to them, and that's being on the complex side. No matter what product or services you're selling, you want to make things easier by covering all of the details that your customers don't have time for. Take all of that hassle out so that nobody else has to worry about it. That's really the point.

We don't just take care of the complexity, we market it. We want to show customers that we have a handle on everything that they might encounter, good and bad. Do you know about the shower system on the Canada cross-country train?

And here's a big one: what about tipping? You'll need to tip your cabin steward and tip the waitstaff, but you have two sets of crew and staff along the way, because they get off the train halfway and a new crew comes on. There are no ATMs on the train, so you need enough cash to bring. Now, many places (especially these days) allow for electronic tipping, but it's good to be prepared.

How can we make all of this complexity easy for our customers? Well, here's your checklist. Everything is set ahead of time so when they are underway, they know it's all taken care of. It's ease of use that keeps customers happy and keeps them coming back.

Those are some examples of what we think about from a marketing perspective. We do market some of the complexities so that when the customer sees what we offer, in addition to just selling the trip, they say to themselves, "Why don't we just use them? Because they take care of it." We offer a one-stop service and take away all the hassle. That's being on the complex side, dealing with all those complexities, so the customer can just take their trip and enjoy it.

With travel in general, whether it's our type of travel or any business, customers come to it or go to travel advisors who are selling our product. Remember, they're not just at different stages, they have many different questions at different stages. Some customers are completely new and don't know where to start, but we also have customers that are much farther along. They've researched their trip, maybe they've even been to the destination before, and reaching out to us is the last piece of it. Others might finally be getting to go to Italy, or what have you. We might have some people that have no idea what to do and need our immersion in the complex to help them along.

They are earlier in the stage or they may have seen a nice hotel somewhere, and want to stay there in this one particular city. Or perhaps they saw this location in a movie (it happens!) and want to build a trip around that experience. Or maybe they love wine and want to visit vineyards and wineries to taste. Maybe someone wants to go truffle hunting. It might be a very particular request that we have to work backward from, so we need to have that flexibility, to accommodate what anyone might want and need.

Customers come to us at different stages of their travel plans, and we want to help them, no matter where they are in the process. They might have very different reasons for taking similar trips and we have to take that into consideration when we market the complexities. When someone sees all the different kinds of customers we have, even if they're going to the same destination, we want them to see themselves.

SPEED-SIMPLICITY-SCALABILITY

LET'S SAY WE HAVE SEVERAL NEW STAFF MEMBERS coming in, but they're all on the East Coast of the United States. Okay, but how are we supporting our Australian staff and customers, for example? Or wherever there might be a need? We always need to think about where our greatest needs are. Yes, we'll have more staff as we grow, but sometimes, we don't need as many if we think strategically about where they're located.

With a worldwide staff, we've extended the workdays. This kind of constant service can be true of something like a call center, but we've extended it to all our other departments. This is critical, whether it's the accounting department, or somewhere else. The interaction between our customers and travel advisors with us is dynamic. Being a remote company now, this is great, because our back-end departments are so integrated with our front-end departments that the service level between them is high. We don't have to say, "I'll get back to them tomorrow." First of all, tomorrow might be too late!

Our customer patterns are always changing, so our global positioning can really help meet their needs. We might have a booking from Australia going to Europe and they are traveling in thirty days, which was previously almost unheard of. Or, they might call and book today, wanting a trip that's two years out. The journey of each customer, and even every travel agency, is very different.

Someone might be going to a conference and have a few extra days afterward, so they want to add a last-minute trip somewhere nearby. We can accommodate this, where many companies don't accept last-minute bookings, because it's just too hard for them to do operationally. We can offer rail tickets, hotel rooms, even in multiple cities. This is a challenge, of course, but as we like to say with a lot of string and duct tape, we can make it work!

Of course, all the seats on the train might be booked up, or all the hotel rooms reserved, so that's when we have to get creative. A lot of these kinds of bookings are often automated, but honestly, sometimes just picking up the phone and calling can yield amazing results. I can call a hotel and ask and they might tell me they have one extra room remaining. You'd be surprised at how often this happens and how simple it can be to reserve it for a customer at the last minute. Hotels and trains both over-sell, so it looks like they have no rooms, but just speaking with a human can often get you the result you want.

They may have sections or rooms reserved but not officially claimed, which allows last-minute shoppers to still find availability. There's the joke about the woman asking her husband if he booked the trip, and he assures her that he did it a month ago, only to get on the phone in a panic and try to book everything at the last minute because he forgot. If that happens, we can be here to save him and maybe his marriage! Those last-minute calls are almost like gold to us, because the customers are already planning to travel, so it's not like they're in the research phase. They need to book the trip and soon.

Thinking about the difference between B2B and B2C for a moment, on the B2C side, we're concerned with customers' questions, emotions, and excitement. They could have read a book, heard that a friend went, have looked online, done some research, and so on. They're excited and they can visualize themselves in that destination. On the B2B side, from a travel agent's standpoint, they're the expert, they're the reseller, so the emotion isn't there, simply because they're not going to that location.

But they still need to pay attention to the customer, and that's where we can help. We see that there are two things we can do that are really important for a travel agent or tour operator: teach them something they don't know and make them look good for their customer. The one thing they're giving us is an opportunity to book with us for their customer. Now, that customer could represent a lot of revenue to an agent; maybe they booked their wedding with them, and now they're considering other trips. The agent is entrusting us with the task and they're trusting us to do a good job, because we're the experts; we're the mechanic on that engine, so we understand how the whole process works. The agent might not, so their needs and questions are very different from our direct consumers.

When I say, "teaching them something that they don't know," part of that is educating them to be able to educate their customer on whatever their next question might be, because we know direct customers. We know how to effectively address objections, for example. But we also want to teach them something they might not know. We might point out on a train trip that some seats face backwards (common on European trains, since trains have to reverse direction for different routes all the time). The customer might not want to sit backwards for several hours on a trip, or we might want to make sure that the customer gets a seat on say, the left-hand side of the train to be able to see a Norwegian fjord better.

This allows travel agents the ability to deliver these kinds of services to their customers with knowledge and confidence. It improves the customer's experience and builds trust between a customer and the agent, and between the agent and us. Remember: *if a customer is spending their hard-earned money on the trip of a lifetime, you need to deliver!*

Obviously, we take different approaches between B2B and B2C customers, since they have different needs, and each has to be met in different ways and even on their own terms. We might work with a travel agent who is a European specialist, or a Scandinavian specialist, for example, and their customers will have specific needs, so we need to help them facilitate the sale.

On the other hand, someone might come to us directly. Maybe they've visited dozens of countries and know the score, or maybe it's their first trip and they just don't want to drive anywhere in an unfamiliar environment. We will sketch out scenarios for them, almost like characters in a play, and we'll go through a series of qualifying questions with both a travel agent and a direct customer to adjust our presentation based on their knowledge. Some might have a lot of knowledge about train travel, while others know nothing.

When we do work with travel agents, there's a real pressure to get it right because they're trusting us, and if we mess up something they won't use us again; it really is that simple.

Obviously, that puts real pressure on us to have to get everything right. A travel agent needs repeat bookings (which represent a lot of revenue), but getting that first booking from a new customer can be the hardest part. It's important to keep in mind that when we market our company to an agent, we need to convince them to go with us, and that means getting everything right, doing a good job, and taking care of their customer. We're asking them to take a chance on us, based on our reputation, reviews, etc., and that can be a difficult sell. A success will be a success for everyone, a failure could lead to bigger problems and never having the chance to work with that agent again.

We're always very thankful to our travel partners for giving us a chance and we don't take it for granted even now, regardless of our size, because we still have to deliver for their customers. I'm hypersensitive to that. And let's be honest, things go wrong even on the best-planned trip. A train might break down, a hotel might have a fire; things happen, so we have to be ready to pivot. I need to think at any given moment about how to fix things if a problem comes up: a cancelled train, a major delay, a rail strike, etc. We have to be ready to rebook a customer and to communicate with their travel agent about what's going on, keeping them in the loop. The customer will reach out to them on their own, so it's better if the agent is prepared and even has extra information.

Different markets rise or stabilize at different times. It might happen that a destination all of a sudden becomes super popular. Certain destinations will do well all the time, such as Italy or Switzerland, but then all of a sudden, Scandinavia or Canada might take off. We always need to be ahead of these trends and aware of what each place has to offer. Often, these trends are customer-driven. They found something online, researched it, and so on, and now they want to know if we can get them there. In some cases, they're almost travel agents themselves!

So, of course, we have to keep our travel partners (agents, hotels, and more) in the loop, and we need to make sure they are as flexible about these changes as we are. We try to choose partners who are knowledgeable and flexible in their own ways. When choosing partners, we look at a given destination first, because we might only have a limited number of potential partners to work with, for example, national parks in the United States. There are obviously only a very limited number of hotels we can work with in these locations, whereas other areas might have many more choices. We look at a given hotel's location, its rating, its closeness to conveniences, transportation options, and so on. Then we look at the service side. We get reports back from our customers about where there's good levels of service. Lastly, we want to determine which partners will support us the most in terms of marketing and availability. If a hotel never has any rooms available, what would be the point of partnering with them?

We want to know that they are engaging with us and taking care of our customers. Are the customers enjoying their experience at the property? Does the hotel want to actively work with us to secure good room rates and availability? Will they send reps to our summit conference? Are they giving us marketing support? A hotel has to provide something for us, too, or it's not worth our time to work with them.

Many hotels are relying more and more on the leisure side of travel, since conferences and business travelers at hotels dropped off significantly during COVID-19. Conferences have come back strongly, but business travel is probably less than before the pandemic, simply because more people got used to having remote meetings via Zoom and other platforms. People are simply not traveling as much for business as they used to. It's become more of a hybrid thing, with some travel, but a lot more people are doing remote transactions.

Business travel is more difficult, simply because if you want to travel to meet someone at another company, they might only be in the office on certain days, and you will have to coordinate your schedules to make sure they match up. It's kind of funny to travel to some place, and then you end up just meeting on Zoom at that location, anyway!

While we do get asked about our decision to switch to all-remote, we feel that we have to commit to this change. The world changes rapidly, and we're just trying to keep up. Companies need to adapt quickly, and a lot of them aren't really doing so. There is still this intransigence about change. It can be nerve-wracking, to be sure, and you never know what will work and what won't, but you have to try.

If I'm concerned about something, I share those concerns with the whole team; I try to be very open about it. Then, we'll have breakout sessions, where we ask questions and collaborate on solutions, and because this is remote work, it has its challenges. Learning can be slower, simply because you're not right next to someone, where you can spark ideas off of each other and brainstorm.

And of course, everything overlaps with technology. Our embrace of new technology is across the board; it has to be. We measure early; sometimes when we create a new tech process, it works, and sometimes not. We might try it for a month and then our analyst will report on it to let us know if it's working. If not, we "fail" quickly with it. We don't want to just have it because it's new. If it's not working for us, we're fine with ditching it for something that suits us better.

Sometimes, it's simply that human beings do a better job than the tech that in theory is going to replace them. Technology can be overwhelming because there is so much out there, and something new is always coming along. We have to look at it end-to-end, and decide if it's worth our time and investment. Most importantly, is it actually faster and better for the customer? Sometimes, we have so much technology to update that it's actually slowing us down in the grand scheme of things. It might look pretty, but it actually isn't helping us or our customers at all.

We then take out the tech and put a human in its place because it's just too slow, and ironically, a human can do the job more efficiently and better. For example, we use a lot of APIs (application programming interfaces), which is just a way for two or more computers or their programs to communicate with each other. It's getting a direct pipeline into something, say from Hilton's inventory system to our reservations; we can dip right in and grab what we need.

However, we've occasionally found it necessary to remove certain APIs. For example, maybe we have one for sightseeing tours in Rome. That would be fine, but it might only allow booking that tour a maximum of sixty days prior, because the vendors use the API to dump their inventory sixty days at a time. That kind of setup actually hurts us, because now we have thousands of customers who have to wait until sixty days before their tour to book it. That's not good for them or us, and we're kind of screwing ourselves by staying with it. If we have, say, 20,000 people but only sixty days to book, you can see how that can cause huge problems! So, we'll dump that API and take bookings manually, because then we can take them well in advance of sixty days. What seemed like a great idea in application (automating bookings) ends up creating more problems than if we just apply the human touch.

We have other examples of where we've brought in a new technology, but the amount of time it takes to use it, whether learning it, or in the ease of use, just killed more time in the bigger picture of what we trying to do. It's better off if we just do it ourselves!

When I was giving my speech at the 2024 Railbookers Group Global Summit, I looked around at everyone there, and I said, "Look at how many different countries you're all from. All these different cultures and languages, and look at how different we all are. But there's one thing we are exactly the same on; I don't care if you're in Australia, or America, or Asia, it doesn't matter. The one thing we're all the same on is time. We all wake up with the same twenty-four hours a day. But what we do in that time—what goes in our ears, our eyes, our mouths—separates us from good to great."

And it's really that simple. We run a session on productivity and being on time, and how sometimes the technology is a barrier to that. We have to weigh what's faster and then what's scalable; that's a constant battle for us. We look at tech that says it's faster and will make us more productive. But I might look at it and say, "Yeah, but is it really? And faster for who?"

It might work at one place, but it creates a problem for the next person down the line who's got to work on something related. And now, she's got to start from scratch, because it doesn't help her at all; it only helps the person or team at another position in the process. It has to work for everyone, or it won't work at all.

We have a whole department where all they do is just measure this kind of efficiency between every department, because it's moving and changing all the time due to the number of products and services we're booking. Since we're really an aggregator of thousands of services, at the end of the day, if any of our vendors change their processes, we have to go with their preferred process, but that may cause a domino effect to changing something on our side; it's out of our control. A vendor or partner might adopt some new tech as the way they prefer to operate, but that doesn't work for us. They might want us to book a certain way, but if we're doing, say, 7,000 bookings, we simply can't accommodate that new method.

If we have a partner who changes something in their operations and it just doesn't "plug in" to our way of working (remember, we have thousands of partners that we work with), we might have to get them on the phone and explain the problem. We'll always try to find a workaround, because we want to be as accommodating as possible to all of our vendors and partners. At the end of the day, we want to make it easy for everyone to make money! Sadly, sometimes there isn't a good solution and we have to part ways, because continuing to try to have a workaround would be a detriment to us; it might even slow us down elsewhere in our operations, especially if it takes more time to learn and extra labor to maintain the new system. But often, we can find compromises. This is the great gift and the great curse of technology. There is so much that's new and that is always being introduced, begging to be tried out, to lure us in with its flashy promises.

When it comes to technology of all kinds, we have to balance what works well for us, as well as consider the ever-important human touch. It's a constant struggle in a constantly evolving environment. But what about the elephant in the room that everyone is talking about these days: AI?

AI: THE NEXT CHAPTER IN CUSTOMER EXPERIENCE

AS OF NOW, WE'RE MOVING MORE INTO AI; we have been since October 2023. This topic has taken a lot of our time in that it's created many great discussions about how much technology to use. Let me be clear: AI is *not* going to replace human beings, but we will employ different facets of it, since it speeds up a lot of our processes. There are pieces in the customer journey that are helped with technology and with AI, but there are also pieces that no technology is going to help. You need that human interaction, and we saw that when we were together at the summit.

A lot of companies are rushing into using AI, and we are big believers in it, but we're also seeing it as more of an opportunity to continue to offer the personal touch. We will continue to develop this in the years ahead, always balancing technology with human interaction and personal needs.

At the Summit, I had everyone take the time to think about the best questions to ask customers, travel agents, each other, and other departments. This simple exercise really got everyone thinking; sometimes, the answer is in the question itself, but sometimes people don't know the right questions to ask.

In a recent meeting, we discussed every role in the company. We're adding roles all the time, but now each role is defined by not only the need, but also what is based on our "customer first" policy. We also have to decide literally where in the world that job is needed at the time. That has become such a crucial point for us to keep the machine going 24/7.

We're sometimes asked if we ever worry that we'll have to start letting employees go in the age of AI and automation, or is there always a way to find new roles for them? We have a dedicated team working on this issue. We use AI in all different aspects; I even took a weeklong course at MIT on leading the digital transformation with AI.

What I'm finding is that we can see that some roles will no longer exist, but I'm not saying that the people won't exist, because what I've found is that upskilling someone you need in another area can be just as important as adopting new tech. We don't want AI to be a job-killer.

We use AI in many different aspects today, everything from writing a simple job description to analyzing the Key Performance Indicators (KPIs) and Objectives and Key Results (OKRs) of a given department. We take in a lot of data and upload it, and the computer crunches it, analyzes it, and sends it back. In the past, two or three people might have been doing all of that work, but that doesn't mean we don't need them doing something elsewhere in the company. There are certain skills that we will eventually not need as much (or at all), such as certain kinds of data entry, but we offer so many services and there's no way to do all of that API by automation; someone still has to load it into the system. Also, someone has to check the APIs, because occasionally, they break. Maybe someone needs to know SQL and watch the SQL code; maybe someone needs to learn that code so they can do that task.

Since October 2023, I've had all of our department heads come up with different ideas about AI and other tech topics. They share these thoughts every week: what they're using it for, what they want to do with it, etc. Then we tell the whole company, so the company's getting involved in the process, too.

Inevitably, roles will change, they will evolve, and we want to stay ahead of that often-rapid change. Some roles we won't need anymore, but we're always needing new ones. Lay off too many people and you might just find that when something automated breaks down, you no longer have the people you need to fix it. Companies need to be more careful about this danger going forward. A lot of processes run by themselves, until they don't, and in the rush to save money, some companies might find that they have to spend a lot more in the long run. There's probably a little too much of a romance with AI right now. It's an incredibly useful tool, but it can't replace people.

There's so much more data out there because of social media and all the mobile phones. AI and searches can crawl and grab it all, but it still has to be used in a thoughtful process. We're looking at enterprise level AI that is a closed box, because obviously, we don't want all of our proprietary information out there.

If we put everything out there then people wouldn't need us. We're an aggregator of vital information, so we're also sensitive to the concerns about AI stealing writings and art and repackaging them. It could scrape all our websites and steal a bunch of our text and reword it such that it's presented as original, when they didn't write a word of it; that's a real danger.

Unfortunately, the law is about five steps behind technology most of the time, so politicians have to catch up to try to regulate these things, and by the time they do regulate one thing, we're on to something else. It's going to be a huge problem going forward.

We do have to embrace AI, the good, the bad, and the ugly, but we have to find a way to embrace it while learning as much as we can. People want answers and solutions as fast as possible, even immediately. They want an immediate change to a travel itinerary, or a booking, for example, so how can we deliver that? We can only physically deliver so much, but when we have something as powerful as an AI tool that can aggregate so many data points that we could never do on our own, it offers us a tremendous advantage. We'd be overwhelmed otherwise, and no human being could possibly collect all of that information.

Another thing we use AI for, being a one hundred percent remote company, is that much of our internal communication is done through chat. A lot of useful information and ideas get put out through them. In October 2023, we started having AI do a weekly summary of every group chat. It grabs all the data and summarizes it for our analysts. This has been extremely helpful. The AI will, for example, look for the top ten questions in the chats and list them. Then, we can publish them with answers so that everyone gets to see them. This saves us a huge amount of time and ensures that important ideas don't get lost forever in a sea of endless data. There are thousands and thousands of chat texts and there would be no way for anyone to go through them all.

We launched a new reservation system in 2023, and we're running dual systems right now, so there's a lot of back and forth with any new system as it slowly rolls out. I had our analyst grab everything in the chat system regarding some of the key issues, and I went back to the team that's working on them and asked, "What do you think the number one issue is that people are having with our new system?" They mentioned many different things, but I told them, "Actually it's all of you not getting back to them in a timely manner." They were shocked! They didn't even realize and it hadn't come up in their own discussions. The problem was right in front of their faces but they wouldn't know that.

These examples, to me, show how we can use AI in an ethical way that doesn't threaten jobs; it's just making existing jobs easier, which is what I think AI should do.

The thing that I see, especially with AI coming and technology and digital, is more and more people yearning for the personal touch, whatever that personal touch is. Whether that's pre-, during, post-, or calling and setting it up, we love the speed of digital. We like the quick answers, but we also love that people love personalization.

How do you deliver that? Those little touches? That's the thing that makes the trip unforgettable, especially if you can feel privileged to do something that's a little bit off the beaten path. A tour guide might say, "We don't normally do this, but today we'll show you this, or we'll take you here, or you'll get to see this old building or this old castle; it's open today, so let's go take a look at it." That offers a personalized touch to the trip that wasn't even in their itinerary, but it makes it that much more entertaining and interesting.

I asked our team if we could string together all of our luxury train trips into one grand tour, like those you might see for planes or cruise ships. This led to the creation of our "Around the World by Luxury Train " mega-trip that really does take in the entire world. *Condé Nast Traveler* recommended it as one of their top twenty trips for 2024, and you might be surprised at just how many people have already purchased it! Retirees looking for a three-month trip around the world are a prime market, for example. It gets people thinking; they didn't even know something like this was possible, but it puts the idea in their minds.

One of my sons wanted to go into accounting at college, and I told him he probably shouldn't. I wasn't knocking the profession by any means, but like it or not, most accounting services will probably be automated eventually. I said go for project management instead. It needs a human touch and that is never going away. AI isn't going to be able manage or coach people. There will always be gray areas in business and that's where someone should want to be. A computer can't clear those up, but a human can. Coaching and managing, and anywhere that you need opinions and subjective analysis, will always need to be the province of human work. A machine just won't give you the same results. If someone is having a bad day or an emotional meltdown, for example, you need a human being there to be able to help. Understanding personalities, basic human psychology, human interactions, and managing methods will make someone instantly valuable, even in the face of growing automation.

We approach this when dealing with customers from different parts of the world, and the cultural practices and behaviors they bring with them. We train people on this topic. Someone from New York will probably have a different personality than someone from, say, Minnesota, much less a customer from Japan or elsewhere in the world. We understand this and adjust to them and their needs accordingly. What AI is ever going to be able to work with so many different people?

These days, I get bombarded with emails that are automated, offering services of all kinds. I don't even know what most of these companies do, and no human is actually sending them out, much less personalizing them. I delete them all the time, but they are what's called a trigger email, so if you don't respond, you'll get another, say, a week later, wanting you to fill in a meeting spot on their calendar. I would never work with any of them, because they've all put me on an automated drip list. If someone from one of these companies would actually call me, or reach out in any real, human way, I would actually pass the message on to one of our managers, simply because they took the time to personalize it and took an interest in me and my company. I'm not interested at all if it's just someone who wants to blast a million things out there.

Too many people seem to do this these days. They just decide that they're going to blanket email people without even learning anything about the company, or the business, or anything else. Why don't they take a little time to learn about these companies instead? It's astonishing how many people do this because they want to get things out as quickly as possible and they think they need to get out dozens, or even hundreds of communications. They don't bother to personalize anything, so it's either going in the spam folder or the recipients are just not paying any attention and end up deleting them. Just a little bit of personalization goes a long way.

When you want to reach out to people, learn something about them, tell them why you want to work with them, find out who they are, what their names are, and what you already know. Read through their website, learn about them, and personalize your communications. Why should you two connect? What's in it for them?

These are the questions you need to be asking.

GLOBAL SUMMIT

Being a fully remote company, we knew we had to bring as many of our people together as possible. Today, we have our Railbookers Group Global Summit once a year. We include our staff in combination with our rail, hotel, and sightseeing partners and vendors, along with guest speakers and top travel advisors for a five-day event.

During our Global Summit, we brought in about a third of our staff from six countries and thirty-four states. Some had actually never met each other in person. It truly was an out-of-body experience! The number of hugs and the emotion on display … we'd never seen anything like it! Everyone was buzzing about it for weeks afterward because when they met someone they'd only known online, suddenly that person wasn't one-dimensional anymore. There was a human behind the Zoom screen! And we had the chance to have so many good conversations.

One of the topics that came up a lot during the summit was about the need for careful planning. I reminded everyone that you have to "plan to plan," and so often, people don't plan to plan. I think this idea goes directly to what we do with our customers: we talk about focusing on the customer, and in doing that, we plan to plan about them, whether it's data research, what are they're doing, or any number of other possibilities. We must have the discipline to sit down and listen to them. We ran a session on this topic, too.

Obviously, we are all about customer focus, but where do you start? How do you approach the subject? How are you spending time to do the right things?

We did a session where I said, "Take out a piece of paper and for the next thirty minutes, write down every question you would love to ask." I could see that once they got past the first five minutes, they really started thinking deeply about this. Soon, they started sharing with each other, and all of a sudden it took on another form. I realized that we need to do this on an ongoing basis.

At this summit, I had a half-day session, which I called a "Fishbowl Session." I told everyone to bring their laptops and work together for that half a day. They did what they would normally do, but they worked on things together. Some of them were astonished at the results, telling me it was the best thing they could have done. I walked around in between them and could hear them sharing ideas and getting excited.

Several people asked me if next year's session could be longer, so at the next summit, we did a day-and-a-half Fishbowl Session!

THE FUTURE

WHERE DO WE SEE THE STATE OF THINGS concerning sustainability and the future? Where are we going to be in five or ten years? Where will the industry be? Obviously, technology is a key aspect, and I have to turn to AI and all its controversies once more.

On the AI side, I would say there's a lot of fear around it, and the idea that it's going to replace us, but after learning about it, that's really not the case. AI will give us the opportunity to amplify and do much more than we could before. For us as an organization, we're focused on the customer and the customer's journey, as we've seen. But how does AI help us in every aspect of that customer journey to provide even better service, better information? Where are we starting?

We're starting with every role in the company. In each department, we have a project going on now where we're breaking every role down to tasks. What is the number of tasks that a given role does? Then we ask, what tasks should be done by a machine and what tasks should done by a human? We know jobs will change in the organization, but we're sharing this process with the whole company and they're involved in it. We don't want this to be a fearful thing. I've said to some of our team, "Those of you that copy from here and paste in there, that will go away, but we want to upskill you, maybe to quality control for some of the work that AI does." We're going through that process now on the back end, and also with the whole customer journey, beginning to end, doing the same thing.

What part should be a human? What part should be a machine? What part should be in concert with both?

The thing that I believe in with all technology, is that people will always want the human touch. You simply can't automate everything, so how can you automate to provide a better experience along the way? As we're going through it into the future, we find that there are so many things that can be automated that are just time wasters. So, what can we do to get better service? It's amazing how many creative ideas come out of you when you're looking at what you're going to automate. It's like you free your mind for new ideas and concepts. We realize we don't have to do a certain task anymore. What could we do, instead? And how do we surprise our customers?

Further, how can we use AI and data effectively, to position it in a way that's easier to use? As an example, we're in the process of creating a data lake, because one of the things with AI is you don't need just structured data. So much data is in a given format, even a survey, which might include drop-down data. Surveys are drop-down and the customer selects. But as I've said, the problem is that then you're giving them the answers and you're not getting pure data.

But sometimes your analysts don't like the unstructured data … precisely because it's unstructured! Personally, I love unstructured data, because it's pure; it's people's words from their hearts. But because of how AI can interpret and how it runs through the LLMs (language learning models), it can crunch all that data very quickly.

This allows you now to pull in data that you've never thought of before. As an example, we get thousands of calls every week. We're putting in technology to transcribe the calls, not our staff members, and then we put that into a massive database so we can see and summarize what questions we're being asked on a regular basis.

We want our data as close to the customer as possible and in real time, so we can decide what type of future technology to use, as well as how we respond and how we anticipate changes to things going forward. I'm focused more on the front end, the customer journey, because many companies are focused on the back end. We are too, which is great, but if you put in more volume, that process you just automated went away, and that will change.

If you focus on the front end, it may change how you're doing things on the back end, or you may not even need to work on the back end because you've solved the problem up front.

In early 2024, I enrolled in the MIT Management Executive Education Course "Leading the AI-Driven Organization," led by the incredible Senior Lecturer in Information Technology, Paul McDonagh-Smith. It was an eye-opening, thought-provoking course that has helped enhance our company's direction on AI and human interaction to enhance our customers' experience. It also brought me lifelong friends and classmates. Though it was amazing and educational, I noticed that I was one of the only people in the room talking about customers. During one of our coffee breaks Professor McDonagh-Smith said, "You know you're one of the only ones that mentions the customer, which is very good."

And I said, "Well, I know how we get paid. I know how things work, right? And it's not about what I like. I'm not the customer. They are."

Now, some of the attendees, to be fair, don't deal with end-customers in their fields, and a lot of my core is different, but it's amazing how customer service doesn't come up as much in AI discussions.

But if you could ask your customers anything you wanted at any time, and find out as much about them as you could, what would you ask them? What would you want to know that would help you and them process their order quicker, give them better service, and offer them more products and services? AI can help us do that.

When we have the ability to go through lots of data very quickly, we have to start thinking about it differently, because now we can ask any questions. Really, what would you want to know about your customer? I think approaching the technology that way opens our minds up to what we couldn't do before.

So, what is the future for us? What are we going to do in five years, in ten years, using AI, using other tools? How is the industry going to change? What are we going to do to keep up with it? How is AI going to work with that? What's going to change in the world? Yes, that's a lot of questions!

What we can do is make our services simpler, faster, and easier for anyone to access. So, if everybody can access everything, we have to ask: if someone is a specialist in something, are they a specialist anymore when anyone can get that information? Well, some of that information is going to be incorrect. For example, someone might search for the best rail route in a search engine and get an answer, but we know that railroad doesn't exist anymore. And how would the person searching know that, unless they really dive into it?

So as a business, where do we create value going forward? There are a few areas. Again, we always want to stay in the complex space, meaning if it's simple, it's commodity-based, it's a click away, the potential customer doesn't need anyone, right? We want to make sure that we're positioning ourselves properly and we're in the complex space. We are now, perhaps more than other businesses, but we want to stay there, providing information about multiple rail lines in multiple countries.

We keep evolving the product to deliver great service with great travel experiences, but also focus on the complex side. The more things get automated and the more technology comes up, the more we see a huge opportunity for us to provide the human experience. People don't just want to deal with machines all the time.

You see that everywhere; companies are trying to automate everything. And we're thinking, "Can I please just talk to someone? Can someone just point me in the right direction?"

As an example, I spoke with a number of travel agents at a conference in Santiago, Chile, who resell our products. Some of the travelers and travel reps were coming up to me and saying, "I hadn't heard about your company before. Where have you been my whole life? You guys saved me so much time!"

They had bad experiences with other companies and they were desperate to talk to someone, anyone. And that's because those other companies are technology companies, for the most part; there's actually no one to call.

But we're a tour operator. I said to them, "Let me explain the difference: when you decide to use that company, you work for *them*. When you decide to give us an opportunity, we work for you. That's the difference, because you're the res agent for that company. They're just for technology, and that's why you're getting stuck. There's no one to call. For us, we have someone at the other end that's there to help you, to guide you. We don't expect you to be a doctor and prescribe for yourself, because you're not a doctor. And that's why we exist."

And they would say to me, "I never thought of it like that!"

I said, "Yes, you work for them because they decided to save money. They have technology, but they don't want to touch it."

So, I think for us, it's about finding the right balance with speed, technology, and service in the future, because people do want things immediately. But they also need that human touch and service, to know that we've got their backs whenever they need us. Now, that could all be done electronically. We don't have to talk to customers, we could have them text us or use online chat, but we don't. And that to me is where we want to go to continue to be successful in the future.

We absolutely embrace new technology, one hundred percent, but not to the detriment of the human being, not to the detriment of where we can't give the personal touch. We'll stay in the complex, automate as much as we can for speed, but also retain that human touch.

The new currency is data and information. Who has the right answer and how fast can you deliver it? Also, where do you store your data? How do you serve it up? And of course, we will continue to produce videos that show customers exactly what they will see and where to go.

Say someone is traveling from Rome to Florence by train. Well, I want you to have a five-second, ten-second, thirty-second video of what to expect before you arrive. Have a great time; this is what the train station looks like or this is where you're going , so by the time you get to the station, it's not the first time you've seen it. We'll show you exactly what to do and where to go. That's what I mean about data in the future. Whatever content and data there is, that's the new currency. Because if I can serve it up quickly, I can make the whole experience easier for you.

What about the overall future of the travel industry, then, and how we fit into it? What trends will be important?

I love the space we're in currently, and I'm so thankful. I think it's limitless for us. And I think it's only going to get bigger and bigger. One key thing with rail is that it's much bigger than most people think, meaning that in most cases, the infrastructure is already in place. Again, there are over 26,000 stations in Europe, there are 500 stations in the US, and 400 in Canada. This means that for people looking for a travel alternative, it's all laid out for them. It's easier than flying, it's more relaxing than driving, and the appeal of that freedom will only grow. More and more places are becoming accessible by train, and an increasing number of people want to adventure and travel out. And the train is an easier, simpler way.

We see other countries continuing to build new rail lines and putting a lot into that infrastructure. There are also different types of rail. There is a resurgence in Europe of bringing back sleeper trains, and we see more luxury trains running again. We're also seeing more and more river cruising, which comes from a similar attitude (skip the car or plane, let someone else do the "driving," and see the sights).

In our opinion, the view from the plane always looks the same, and the view from the big cruise ship at times might be the same, but the view from the train is always different, and that's what makes rail travel interesting. It's the different places and things you get to see.

When I look to the future, I don't see an end to that attitude, that desire for exploration. There will be different opinions over time: Oh, this country's not popular right now, or that destination is boring, but rail travel will only become more popular.

What about the US rail system? Will it ever get up to speed? We operate vacations for Amtrak, but I'd say that the thing with the US compared to other places, such as Europe, is that we have natural challenges. The biggest, of course, is distance. While there are a lot of cities close to each other in the US, there are many more that are far away from each other.

So, to build up bigger rail networks in the US is a much greater investment. At the end of the day, it's still up to Congress to pass legislation for funding, and that's a slow burn. It takes a while for these things to come up. While there are private companies trying to bid on certain routes, it's still a challenge. There are some new investments in routes from the Northeast to the Northwest, but it's not happening nationwide.

Despite this, Amtrak still moves almost thirty million people a year. It's bigger than people realize, but it takes that commitment to investment. While European and other countries fund their rail lines through government spending, it's not the same in the US. The UK deregulated, but that's why UK rail is so expensive. The companies are trying to make money on it, and they have specific routes.

For the US, Amtrak is the only rail company. So how much marketing are they doing? Potential customers only know about where they live, and maybe where their station is, but they often don't know where else the lines go, and that's always the number one challenge. When I talk to people about going to the Grand Canyon, or Glacier National Park, they're amazed that they can do it by train. They might, for example, only think of trains going between Boston and New York, or maybe Chicago to St. Paul, Minnesota and from their local area.

Now, as far as sustainability, train is the second-best way to travel for sustainability besides walking or riding a bike. And sustainability is becoming more important (as we've seen, France is limiting in-country flights).

To be honest, at the moment, very few customers buy from us because of sustainability. They like the fact that it's there, but they're really looking for a good vacation deal. And typically, they had to fly to their destination (such as from America to Europe), and maybe drive their car to the airport first, or get a shuttle. They do, however, like the fact that the train removes stress and is more sustainable.

Sustainability is important and only becoming more so as it becomes a larger part of the conversation. I think tying sustainability with ease of travel makes it easier to accept.

Honestly, we're probably one of the most sustainable companies. No one commutes and we print nothing; everything is digital. We have a very low output of pollution or garbage, or anything else.

What about our growth and expansion as a company? It's still happening and at an impressive rate. It's an exciting and interesting phenomenon. Being fully remote, we are always growing and always adding staff. Again, we have the advantage of hiring the best wherever they're from, because we're not restricted by a location.

We're also specific on every role in the company. That way, we can keep the machine going even if it's the internal customer support. This process has really been fun and exciting, because we're rethinking a business model based on something remote. If we can have that position in Australia, and someone's contacting them from the US on Sunday, well, now someone is working because it's already Monday there. Now, things can be ready for the team in, for example, London, to start on their next morning. This allows for information to go out faster for the customer, and they can get answers to any specific questions. Or, suppose there's an emergency; someone can be on it right away.

I receive a lot of calls every week from other people, often leaders that run companies, and they keep asking me, "How are you doing that?"

And I tell them, "The whole thing is remote. We still get together. We have familiarization trips for our staff to experience our rail vacations with their colleagues from around the world. We also get together at our Railbookers Group Global Summit once a year." We've got amazing staff, and the level of support they give the company and me is almost to a religious cult level (I'm joking!), because they get to stay home. I believe that's really helped our growth because we've got such passionate staff.

I would hope this kind of model would inspire some other companies to consider doing it themselves. Here's our success story, so maybe some other companies should try it. It would be great if we actually did have that kind of influence in this industry and in other industries, as well.

So, where will our company be in five years? Obviously, I'd like for us to be opening up more markets. Not long ago, we opened up New Zealand, for example, and we'd like to do more. I'd like to open up to more markets in new places in Europe and in Asia. I would like more staff focused on the customer journey and less staff just focused on the backend manual side of things.

With rail travel in general, because it means something different to everyone, there's not a lack of leads and there's not a lack of inventory. We don't have something in warehouses for sale, or cabins in a cruise ship that sell out. Most of the time, we can offer any date, any place, any train, and there are tons of trains. We don't have a lack of leads or a lack of inventory. So how can we connect everything? We're working on that technology-wise; faster service, both human and automated, but still offering world-class service.

And that's where I'd like us to be in five years, to know we had a problem at some level and solved it; we mastered it, we made it easier. And to know that we've really expanded in different places where people have the joy of travel. Let's be honest, we sell memories. People go on trips and come back with experiences for a lifetime, and they want to share those with their friends and loved ones, and it's a privilege to be a part of that.

Our mission is to continue to be the largest flexible independent travel (FIT) rail vacation packager in the world, while providing world-class service. We have an openness, a passion for growing and evolving, and not just sitting on what we know and the experience we already have. It's taken us to some amazing places, from that one East Coast office to a worldwide presence. We became much bigger than many of us would have guessed! We always knew our company would be successful, but some of us had no idea just how much. Over the past decade or so, there has never been one year with the company that has been identical to the year before. We've never just gone through the motions. We've learned from what didn't work, and taken the things that have worked and committed ourselves to making them better in the next phase. That practice hasn't slowed down, and that's what we see as the future of Railbookers. We're always excited for the company and where we're going. We can promise that there's never a boring day at the office!

And I'm very grateful. It's amazing to wake up in the morning thinking, "Wow, I get to do this, that's really cool!" as opposed to doing something I hate. People love travel, and we can help spread that love.

We're not selling cups, we're not selling widgets, we're not selling tires. We're selling something that's inexhaustible, and that's great, because there's always more of it to sell. We don't keep train trips in a warehouse somewhere. Every day, we have an endless supply of them that we can offer to people, and that's great for building on the future. And that's how I get inspired and excited. With both customers and the services that we provide, it's limitless on both ends; how many businesses have that?

Limitless opportunity, customers, and inventory. The future looks great!

ACKNOWLEDGMENTS

I WOULD LIKE TO THANK MY WIFE, **Molly**, and my twin sons, **Roan** and **Vance**, for their unwavering support in my career and letting me always just be a husband and father when I take the cape off.

To my partner in crime and business partner, **John Tavano**. Thank you for your complete support in letting me be myself, and for the remarkable journey we are on.

To my brother **Jim**, our Senior Vice President of Sales, who has the worst job in the world: working for his older brother. Thanks for always supporting me and being the Energizer Bunny of our company.

To our RBG management team and long-term employees, thank you for believing in me even when you thought my ideas were crazy.

To my mentors who have guided my business career and always encouraged me: **Dan Sullivan**, **Dave Hosking**, **Richard Launder**, **Brett Tollman**.

Finally, thank you to our amazing customers and travel advisors. If not for you, we wouldn't be here. You are truly our CEOs. Thank you.

ABOUT THE AUTHOR

FRANK MARINI is the President and CEO of Railbookers Group, where he oversees the company's global travel brands, Railbookers and Amtrak Vacations. In his role, Marini is responsible for the strategy, growth, operations, and performance of all Railbookers Group brands.

Prior to his current position, Marini served in several leadership roles, notably as Vice President of Sales for Collette Vacations, and as President of Contiki Holidays, a Travel Corporation company.

Marini has been featured in *Travel Weekly*, *TravelAge West*, *Travel Agent*, *Agent@Home*, and *Recommend* magazines, and is a frequent speaker at industry-related events. Accolades include being named a leading executive in OC Metro's "40 under 40," as well as an honoree of the annual "Top 40 Under Forty" by *Providence Business News* which recognizes the next generation of business community leaders. He has also received the Travvy Award for the "Most Innovative Executive, Rail Travel."

Marini has served on the Board of Directors for the Pawtucket YMCA, the Rhode Island Chapter of the American Heart Association, and the Boys & Girls Club in Anaheim, California. Currently, Frank serves as a member of the board of the World Travel & Tourism Council as well as a member of the US Travel Association.

Marini holds a bachelor's degree from the University of Rhode Island. He lives in Southern California with his wife and twin sons.